Justice Undone

The Vanishing Pillars of Truth

By
Sydney Crackower

Justice Undone

The Vanishing Pillars of Truth

Table of Contents

Introduction

In a world where change is the only constant, the perception and application of justice face a relentless tide of transformation. As we stand at this crossroads, it's critical to assess what's at stake within our legal systems and why the conversation about justice is more imperative than ever. With every development, the foundation of justice, once deemed immutable, encounters erosion, necessitating a unique and focused examination from concerned citizens, legal scholars, and policymakers.

The legal systems we rely on are the lifelines that maintain societal order and provide a sense of security. Yet, these systems are not immune to the pressures applied by technological advancements, social evolution, and political shifts. How do we ensure that these pressures don't compromise the core principles of justice? That's the question this book seeks to unravel, illuminating the consequences and challenges that follow such rapid changes.

The world today is characterized by a wealth of information at our fingertips—yet as access to information has burgeoned, so too have the intricacies of discerning truth from fiction. Legal systems, fundamentally reliant on the establishment of truth, now find themselves grappling with an unprecedented volume of information, much of which is tainted with misinformation. This blurring of truth doesn't just inhabit the fringes; it has seeped into courtrooms and legislative halls, leaving a trail of uncertainty that we're obliged to address.

Moreover, the relationship between society and its justice systems is symbiotic, constantly evolving as each influences the other. As society grows more complex, so too do its legal structures. However, it's not solely societal shifts that alter the landscape of justice. External forces such as technology and media play pivotal roles in shaping perceptions and public trust. The credibility of our legal institutions is at risk if they can't adapt effectively to these new realities.

Globally, legal systems are far from uniform, yet the challenges they face often bear striking similarities. Different countries present varied approaches and experiences with justice, offering a rich tapestry of lessons and cautionary tales. By casting a global gaze, we can appreciate the nuances and emerge with a broader understanding--a necessity if we're to craft sustainable solutions to seemingly localized issues.

In recent years, the digital revolution has completely disrupted traditional paradigms. Technology's fingerprints are all over courts and legal precedents, presenting both opportunities for greater justice and challenges in consistency and reliability. Artificial intelligence, while a potential tool for efficiency and fairness, also raises questions about biases and oversight. There's a dynamic tension at play, one that invites careful scrutiny and deliberate action.

Political influences further complicate the integrity of legal systems. The intersection of law and politics is a delicate dance, often dictated by agendas that may not prioritize justice above all else. This interplay not only affects the creation of laws but also their implementation and enforcement, sometimes casting shadows over the processes meant to be transparent and equitable. By understanding this intersection, we can start outlining paths to mitigate undue interference.

Justice is not blind to the social context in which it operates. Inequities exist, and these often manifest starkly within legal systems designed to treat all equally. Yet, the reality diverges significantly from the ideal, with unequal access to justice and socioeconomic disparities playing considerable roles in shaping outcomes. Recognizing these issues is the first step towards rectifying them—through education, advocacy, and systemic reform.

Awareness without action is futile. As we unpack the conditions of our current legal systems, the urgent need for activism and reform becomes apparent. From grassroots movements to structured policy initiatives, change is both a possibility and a necessity. This moral imperative is driven by both a commitment to equity and a pragmatic understanding of the evolving legal landscape.

Ultimately, our goal is not merely to critique but to rebuild—to restore the credibility and functionality of justice systems globally. This task is neither simple nor singular; it requires collaborative efforts, innovative thinking, and a steadfast dedication to principles of fairness and transparency. Through this restoration, we aim to renew not just systems, but the public's faith in them.

As we proceed with this exploration, it's crucial to keep an open mind, questioning assumptions and challenging norms. Whether you're a citizen vested in societal well-being, a legal scholar probing the depths of jurisprudential dilemmas, or a policymaker committed to crafting effective laws, the journey to understanding and addressing these changing dynamics of justice is one we must undertake together. Our actions today shape the justice of tomorrow, and together, we hold the power to ensure it is just and righteous.

Foreword: The Foundations of Justice

When pondering the concept of justice, we find it to be less a stationary monument and more a dynamic stream, constantly shaped and reshaped by the fabric of society. Justice is an ideal that serves as a mirror, reflecting the ethos and values of the time. Its foundations are not merely built on statutes but are embedded in the collective consciousness, challenged by both external forces and internal evolution. This foreword seeks to elucidate why the foundations of justice are imperative to the health and progression of any society, while acknowledging the forces that threaten to undermine them.

Justice, at its core, is interwoven with truth and fairness. These pillars support the integrity of legal systems worldwide. But, let us not forget that justice is not only what is enacted within courtrooms, nor is it confined to shelves of law books. It emerges in the minds of those who demand it, in the voices that speak out against its absence, and in the hands of those who uphold it. A society's reverence for justice reveals much about its priorities and its future. Without a steadfast commitment to maintaining justice's foundations, the very blueprint of civilization risks dereliction.

The pursuit of justice is laden with obstacles. History unambiguously displays moments where the scales tipped, not under the weight of evidence, but under the burden of bias, corruption, and misinformation. These are not anomalies to be dismissed lightly. They spotlight the fragility of justice and emphasize the need for vigilance.

As we survey historical precedents, lessons emerge—sometimes in stark opacity—that remind us justice is as vulnerable as it is noble. Thus, to comprehend the architectures that hold justice aloft is to protect it from erosion.

Our era faces unprecedented challenges. The proliferation of information—and misinformation—can either illuminate truth or obscure it. In this rapidly changing landscape, the role of justice is being reevaluated, causing ripple effects that question its application and fairness. As concerned citizens, scholars, and policymakers, we're tasked with taking a proactive stance. Rather than allowing justice to morph uninhibitedly, let's be the architects who refine and reinforce its structure to withstand modern pressures.

However, this endeavor is not solely the purview of legal professionals and lawmakers. It involves a collective societal effort, one that requires comprehension and cooperation from all corners—from educators to everyday citizens. Education becomes paramount in fostering a populace that not only understands the mechanisms of justice but is also willing to challenge and reform them when necessary. Empathy, knowledge, and engagement are tools as formidable as any legal precedent in safeguarding justice's integrity.

To embark on this journey of understanding, one must appreciate the rich tapestry that defines justice's past and present. A multifaceted dialogue is essential as we strive to harmonize history's teachings with future imperatives. Through this discourse, we gain the perspective needed to identify what must be preserved at the foundation and what demands renovation. By establishing a shared commitment to truth, equity, and transparency, we set the stage for justice that is resilient and adaptive.

The chapters that follow this foreword will delve into various aspects of these themes, offering insights and analyses that are crucial for anyone deeply concerned with the state and future of our legal systems. May this introduction serve as both a call to awareness and a pledge towards actionable change. Let's immerse ourselves in the conversation with a readiness to rebuild and rethink. In doing so, we'll find that the foundations of justice do not merely support the law; they embody the hope and integrity of the society they serve.

Erosion of Legal Principles

The very fabric of our legal system, once a bedrock of societal order and justice, is experiencing a subtle yet pervasive erosion. This phenomenon, which we term the erosion of legal principles, underscores a significant yet often overlooked trend in our contemporary world. As we navigate the complexities of modern society, we must confront a reality where foundational legal concepts are being challenged, reshaped, and sometimes abandoned altogether. This is not just a concern for legal scholars or policymakers. It's a critical issue that every concerned citizen must grapple with. After all, the principles of justice affect how we live, govern, and, ultimately, how we understand right from wrong.

At the heart of legal principles lies truth, a concept that has guided the rule of law for centuries. However, this truth is under siege, distorted by misinformation and challenged by the intricacies of verifying facts in a digital age. The ripple effects touch every aspect of the justice system, from courts to public perception. When truth becomes relative, the law loses its grounding, turning from a source of justice into a tool that can be manipulated. We must ask ourselves: what's left of the law when its foundational principles begin to erode?

The historical context of legal systems showcases a timeline of evolution and adaptation to societal needs. In ancient times, laws were pronounced through tradition or divine commands, presenting an ever-changing tapestry that has somewhat remained resilient over centuries. Yet, today's society presents challenges so unique and swift that the legal frameworks struggle to keep pace. Whether through technological advances or shifting political landscapes, the stress on legal systems today is unlike any uprising previously encountered in history.

Public perception plays a crucial role in maintaining the sanctity of these principles. Trust in legal institutions is arguably at an all-time low, fueled by a relentless media cycle that blurs the line between truth and speculation. As these narratives shift public trust, the challenge remains for legal systems to adapt while holding onto their core tenets of fairness, objectivity, and justice. If the public loses confidence, the legal system's authority and relevance are inevitably compromised.

Globally, this erosion isn't happening in isolation. Different countries grapple with similar challenges, albeit in diverse contexts. International perspectives provide both cautionary tales and hopeful models of resilience. We must examine and understand these global narratives to draw relevant lessons for our justice systems. Such comparative analysis highlights how interconnected our global legal community has become—and how shared solutions can lead to reinforced legal frameworks across borders.

Technology is a double-edged sword in this narrative. While it offers tools for efficiency and access, it also disrupts traditional precedents and introduces new risks for the age-old practice of law. Digital evidence introduces complications that can skew justice if not handled with precision. Even more pressing is the role of artificial intelligence, which looms large over courtrooms as a tool market with both great promise and profound ethical dilemmas. As technology evolves, so must our understanding and applications of principles that protect justice's integrity.

Political influence further muddies these waters. Legal integrity often finds itself on uneasy footing when politics casts its shadow. When the objectives of law and politics become conflated, the erosion of principles quickens—a cautionary tale as old as democracy itself. Through case studies, these are not just theoretical musings but real implications affecting the fairness and impartiality of legal outcomes.

Then there is the issue of social inequality. There's the challenge of unequal access to justice, an age-old issue that today magnifies in scope. The socio-economic disparities amplify this divide, placing urgent demands on reformative measures. Without a system that serves all its citizens equitably, the very notion of justice becomes selective and skewed. This erosion is particularly evident in how different communities experience law enforcement and legal representation, amplifying their vulnerabilities instead of alleviating them.

Education emerges as a powerful tool for counteracting the drift away from fundamental legal principles. By educating future legal practitioners and promoting public legal literacy, it's possible to create a well-informed populace that both respects and challenges the legal system constructively. Knowledge empowers citizens to uphold justice and ensures that as legal challenges evolve, the response is equally robust and enlightened.

Finally, activism and reform present avenues for addressing these multidimensional challenges. Grassroots movements and policy initiatives serve as conduits, channeling the citizens' voice into constructive change. These are living proof that legal principles are not static but can be reclaimed and reinvigorated through collective action and reform. When citizens and lawmakers come together, even the most eroded principles can find new strength.

In essence, while the erosion of legal principles is daunting, it is not an inevitability. Through awareness, informed debate, and collective action, it's possible to halt and even reverse this erosion. It requires a concerted effort—a renewed commitment to the principles that secure justice not only for today but for generations to come. As guardians of justice, the task lies with us all to restore these principles to their rightful place as the unshakeable foundation of our legal system.

Chapter 1:
The Role of Truth in Law

In the towering edifice of justice, truth serves as the cornerstone. Without it, the entire structure teeters on the brink of collapse. At its essence, the law is supposed to be a guardian of truth—a beacon guiding the ship of society through tumultuous waters. But more often than not, truth gets tangled in the web of human affairs, clouded by rhetoric and distorted by self-interest. In today's world, the stakes are particularly high. We find ourselves at a crossroads where the integrity of legal systems hangs in the balance, and truth lies at the heart of this precarious juncture.

The law might be an intricate web of rules, statutes, and procedures, but it derives its true power from being an instrument for discovering the truth. Every legal endeavor—be it a trial, an investigation, or a simple negotiation—hinges on the pursuit of truth. Truth fuels justice because only by ascertaining what really happened in any given case can a fair and just resolution be achieved.

Consider the jury, acting as the society's proxy, trying to discern facts from an often muddy soup of narratives. The jury faces not just the task of sifting through facts but of ensuring that their conclusions remain grounded in reality. They are the human link in a chain that can sometimes seem more befitting a Möbius strip, with truth elusive and justice seemingly out of reach. Their job is daunting precisely because it requires not just an examination of evidence but also an appraisal of credibility, intent, and context—all under the watchful gaze of truth.

Yet, in the hustle of litigation and the haze of courtroom maneuvers, truth sometimes takes a backseat. Lawyers, entrusted with the task of advocacy, may stretch or veil the truth under the guise of zealous representation. This can lead to an insidious erosion of legal integrity. When advocacy becomes more about winning than telling the truth, the whole system can suffer.

The courts—our arenas of justice—must not become places where truth is optional or negotiable. However, the reality often begs to differ. Legal battles can turn into spectacles where high-stakes adversarial gamesmanship becomes the focal point. It's a dangerous prospect, blurring the line between truth and professional narrative crafting. As citizens, we should be alarmed by this trend, wary of a system that allows truth to become a casualty of cunning rhetoric.

It's vital to affirm that the law should not merely legislate against lies but actively promote a culture where truth is valued, protected, and incentivized. Legal reforms must focus not just on deterring falsehood but on nurturing avenues that facilitate and reward truth-telling. This requires rethinking current practices that might inadvertently skew incentives away from the truth.

Technology, though often criticized, can be an ally in this endeavor. By deliberately integrating new tools—such as digital forensics, transparent data systems, and objective verification processes—we open the door to innovative pathways that cement the role of truth in the justice system. However, technology's role needs careful regulation to avoid misuse and ensure it remains a servant of truth and not its rival.

Truth in law is not merely about facts; it's also about principles and values. Upholding truth means respecting the foundational ideals of fairness, equity, and justice that underpin our society. This extends beyond the courtroom and into every facet of the legal process, melding with ethics, professional responsibility, and public policy considerations.

We find ourselves at an inflection point. The role of truth in law is under scrutiny, caught in a tug-of-war between time-honored principles and modern pressures. We are called to respond—not with resignation but with determination, fueling a robust dialogue on how truth can regain its rightful place in the legal systems worldwide.

Through concerted effort and vigilant advocacy, we can strive towards a justice system that truly honors truth, rendering it not just a concept but an unquestionable cornerstone of law. This pursuit demands vigilance, courage, and, above all, an unwavering commitment to preserving the integrity of truth as we navigate the complexities of modern legal challenges.

Chapter 2:
Historical Context of Legal Systems

To grasp the complexities of today's legal challenges, we must take a step back and understand the historical trajectory that has shaped modern legal systems. Our shared human history is the engine that has driven the legal structures we see today, complicated as they may be. In essence, every court verdict, legislative amendment, or public protest is part of a long and varied narrative—a tapestry interwoven with cultural evolutions and societal demands.

From the ancient codes of Hammurabi to the nuanced legal principles of the Roman Empire, these early frameworks set a foundational tone, full of both wisdom and complexity. The Romans, particularly, were pioneers, harmonizing diverse legal ideas that allowed their laws to resonate across a vast empire. Their principles not only addressed individual grievances but also underscored the importance of state authority, inadvertently laying down a blueprint still in use by judicial systems worldwide.

Fast forward to the Middle Ages, where feudalism reigned supreme and justice often rested in the hands of local lords, rather than centralized authority. This decentralization was a double-edged sword, enabling tailored justice in some regions while fostering inequities in others. The Magna Carta in 1215 marked a pivotal moment, as it codified the principle that everyone, including the king, was subject to the law. It became a beacon for liberty and fairness and a precursor to constitutional law.

The Enlightenment period brought about a radical rethinking of legal principles. Philosophers like Locke and Montesquieu emphasized reason and individual rights, challenging monarchic traditions and advocating for systems that represent the people. This era highlighted the emergence of the social contract theory, a profound concept wherein individuals consent to surrender some freedoms to a governing body in exchange for protection of their remaining rights. It is no exaggeration to say these profound ideas set the stage for democratic developments across continents.

The American and French revolutions were defining moments where these Enlightenment ideals were put into practice, underscoring the shift from rigid, hierarchical legal structures to ones that prioritized fairness and equality. The United States Constitution, with its Bill of Rights, aimed to protect individual freedoms while ensuring a functional and equitable legal system. This transformation was influential, serving as an archetype for nations in search of justice.

As economies industrialized, the law adapted to meet new challenges. Labor laws emerged to balance power dynamics between employers and workers, reflecting society's evolving ethical standards. Simultaneously, colonial powers exported their legal codes, embedding Western legal traditions in diverse cultures worldwide. This wasn't a seamless integration; rather, it often led to a collision of tradition and foreign influence, complicating legal developments in these regions.

The 20th century introduced even more complexities. The horrors of two World Wars spurred the creation of international legal frameworks aimed at maintaining peace and addressing humanitarian issues. Institutions like the United Nations and the establishment of international courts represented fledgling attempts at transcending national boundaries to enforce justice on a global scale.

Today, as we navigate a rapidly changing world, we can't ignore the historical underpinnings that guide current legal practices and perceptions of justice. Understanding this historical context isn't a mere academic exercise; it's essential for informed dialogue and effective reform. It's clear that while the arc of history bends towards justice, its path is neither straightforward nor without its actors and influences, both benevolent and malignant.

Thus, knowing the legacy left by our predecessors helps us not only to appreciate the systems we've inherited but also empowers us to engage critically in reimagining them. If there is one lesson history teaches, it's that the systems we build today will either become the ballast or the buoyancy for future generations. The challenge is ensuring that the weight of our decisions favors justice, equity, and progress.

Evolution of Justice Systems

The evolution of justice systems is a saga written over centuries, full of trials, errors, and triumphs. Our journey begins in a time when the idea of law was synonymous with the whims of the powerful. Ancient societies had rudimentary systems, but they often relied on tribal traditions and the discretion of leaders rather than codified laws. With Hammurabi's Code in Babylonia, we see one of the earliest attempts to formalize legal principles—setting standards and consequences for actions. It was a leap forward, yet its application favored societal hierarchy. Justice, as it turns out, has been bound to power since its inception.

Fast forward to classical Greece and Rome, and we witness significant advancements in legal thought. The Greeks introduced democratic principles, where citizens could partake in decision-making processes. It represented a budding shift towards individual accountability and the rule of law. On the other hand, Roman Law set a precedent for legal codification and consistency, concepts essential for the future of justice systems across the globe. We owe much to these entities for the development of foundational legal ideas that underpin modern systems.

However, it wasn't until the Enlightenment that justice systems saw a reinvigoration of these notions. Philosophers like John Locke and Montesquieu championed the separation of powers, a fundamental principle to mitigate abuses of authority. This era emphasized reason and individual rights, ushering in the creation of constitutions and charters that would govern nations and protect citizens from the capriciousness of rulers. Legal reforms rooted in Enlightenment principles gave birth to structures that valued equality before the law and due process.

The transition from monarchies to democratic republics further cemented these ideas. The American and French Revolutions demonstrated profound changes where laws became the people's shield against tyranny. The U.S. Constitution, with its Bill of Rights, exemplified a commitment to protecting individual freedoms, setting a benchmark for emerging democracies worldwide.

Yet, change didn't happen in isolation. Throughout history, local realities shaped legal transformations. Colonialism exported European legal systems to diverse cultures, often leading to hybrid forms that attempted a balance between tradition and imposed structures. This clash of legal ideologies sometimes led to conflicts, as colonial rulers imposed laws that rarely aligned with indigenous customs and values.

The 20th century introduced new complexities with the waves of globalization. As nations specialized and interconnected, the need for legal systems to address transnational issues grew. International organizations like the United Nations emerged, creating frameworks to tackle global problems ranging from human rights violations to climate change. The International Court of Justice and various human rights treaties showcase our collective efforts towards a universal legal ethos.

However, not all evolutions signal progress. The increasing political polarization at the end of the 20th and beginning of the 21st centuries has posed fresh challenges. Ideologies clash within and across borders, testing the resilience of justice systems. The delicate balance between maintaining order and preserving freedoms has become a flashpoint, drawing once more on lessons from history while demanding innovation and adaptability.

In recent decades, technological advancements have profoundly impacted legal systems. The digital age is eroding barriers, allowing for instantaneous communication and the proliferation of information, both accurate and misleading. Tech-driven changes present unique dilemmas for justice systems worldwide, as the nuances of cybercrime, privacy rights, and digital evidence redefine legal landscapes. As legal systems evolve to meet these challenges, they stand at a crossroads—one that could either lead to greater justice or unprecedented surveillance and control.

Contemporary justice systems must also grapple with deep-seated inequalities. Although justice systems have made monumental strides over the centuries, issues of accessibility and fairness remain. These unresolved challenges reflect persistent socio-economic disparities that require systemic reform. It underscores the evolution of justice as not only a historical journey but an ongoing struggle.

So, where does this leave us? The evolution of justice systems is far from over. As society changes, so too must the systems that govern it. We find ourselves in an era that compels us to examine both the past and the road ahead. History shows us that justice systems can evolve for the better, but action is required to propel them beyond their imperfect origins to a more just and equitable future. How we adapt to changing societal needs will eventually define the legacy of our justice systems.

Influence of Changing Societies Legal systems aren't static; they are dynamic entities that shape and are shaped by the societal currents around them. We can trace the roots of today's justice systems back to ancient times, but as societies evolve, so too must the mechanisms for administering justice. Throughout history, justice systems have been a reflection of their times—mirroring values, norms, and even the inequalities prevalent within their societies. As communities become more diverse and globalized, the demand for justice systems to be more inclusive and representative has only intensified.

In the ever-shifting landscapes of modern societies, the challenge lies in balancing continuity with progress. Rapid changes in societal structures due to urbanization, technological advances, and cultural shifts bring about unique challenges and opportunities for legal systems. Take, for instance, the increasing mobility of populations. With it comes a blend of cultural perspectives that challenge traditional notions of justice and fairness. The blending of societal norms asks law to be both a stabilizing force and an adaptive entity, ready to accommodate the novel and diverse needs of its populace.

Moreover, movements advocating for social justice, equality, and human rights have called for legal systems to be more transparent and accountable. These movements ignite change, shaking the very foundations of existing legal frameworks. In response, there is a push toward reform that meets the demands of a more informed and engaged citizenry. However, one could argue that the true evolution of a justice system isn't merely about legislation and courts but about ensuring that every individual feels protected and heard under the law. The drive toward such an inclusive and evolved system reflects society's perpetual quest for fairness and justice.

Chapter 3:
The Decline of Truth in Legal Systems

The foundations of any justice system rest upon the immovable bedrock of truth. Yet, as we stride into an era where misinformation is as prevalent as it is perilous, we must confront a disquieting reality: the decline of truth in our legal systems. It's a trend that's not just concerning but alarming, as it threatens to undermine the credibility of institutions that have long been the guardians of fairness and integrity.

One cannot overlook the ripple effects this decline has catalyzed within courtrooms and legal proceedings. Judges, lawyers, and juries find themselves swamped by a deluge of information, much of which is unreliable at best. These complications exacerbate existing challenges, turning the quest for truth into an arduous journey through a labyrinth of half-truths and fabrications. As misinformation multiplies, so does the difficulty in distinguishing fact from fiction, causing trial outcomes to hang precariously on a shifting scale of probability rather than certainty.

Moreover, the advent and rampant dissemination of inaccurate information has eroded public confidence in the justice system. Trust, once a cornerstone of judicial proceedings, is now treated with skepticism. Citizens, witnessing erroneous narratives spun like silk, question not just individual verdicts but the very institutions meant to uphold justice. This decay in faith is a corrosive agent, weakening the foundations upon which legal systems are constructed.

A critical aspect to examine is how this phenomenon springs from significant shifts in technology and communication. The rise of digital platforms has democratized information sharing, sidestepping traditional gatekeepers who once held misinformation at bay. While this accessibility allows voices to be heard, it also amplifies falsehoods, creating a chaotic cacophony that legal professionals struggle to resolve.

In navigating this complex environment, the challenge of verifying facts becomes glaring. Verification is no longer a matter of ticking off a checklist but demands comprehensive scrutiny of an extensive range of sources. Legal professionals, who once relied on concrete evidence and clear-cut testimonies, now face a digital quagmire of deepfakes and doctored data. The onus of proof is magnified, and the resources needed to combat this barrage are vast and often insufficient.

Despite these formidable obstacles, turning a blind eye is not an option. It's pivotal, more than ever, for stakeholders within the legal domain—be they policymakers, practitioners, or concerned citizens— to rally together with resolve and clarity of purpose. Reinvigorating our legal systems with truth as their guiding principle is an imperative task, one that requires a collective effort to filter and fact-check, ensuring justice is neither spectacle nor sham.

However, it's not only about devising frameworks and bolstering safeguards. There's a pressing need for cultural shifts within and beyond the legal community, encouraging transparency and accountability at every level. Instilling these virtues further edges us toward a future where transparency becomes a contagion, spreading through the echelons of power and governance.

Ultimately, the decline of truth poses a direct challenge to the ethos and efficacy of legal systems worldwide. While the terrain is fraught with difficulties, it's in these exact moments that resilience and reform must carry us through—echoed by the voices of citizens calling for change and leaders emboldened by integrity. Ignoring the symptoms only prolongs the inevitable, but addressing them head-on offers hope for a justice system once more rooted in truth and trust.

The path forward demands commitment, a collective will to restore what's fallen to disrepair. By returning to the roots of factual integrity, restoring public confidence, and embracing transparent practices, there's the promise of a future where the glare of misinformation fades into obscurity. It's a vision that, while ambitious, is within our grasp—if we dare to reach for it.

Impact of Misinformation In our ever-evolving justice systems, misinformation serves as a silent disruptor, quietly but steadily corroding the foundation upon which the pursuit of truth rests. With the digital age's rapid pace and the accessibility of information, both true and false, the dissemination of misinformation has become a formidable challenge for legal practitioners. Our justice systems, traditionally bastions of truth and reliability, now face the daunting task of filtering out inaccuracies from the surging flood of information. The repercussions of failing to do so affect the legitimacy of verdicts, the trust of the public, and ultimately, the evolution of justice systems themselves.

One might recall a simpler time when corroborating facts weren't tied up in the confusing web of digital content. Today, a single piece of misinformation can spread faster than wildfire, reaching vast audiences in an instant. While mistakenly-held beliefs about trivial matters may seem harmless, misinformation related to legal contexts can alter judgments, sway jury opinions, and impede justice. For instance, during high-profile cases, the court of public opinion, fueled by misinformation, can put undue pressure on legal professionals, influencing outcomes that may not align with objective truth.

Furthermore, this plague of misinformation doesn't just affect the courtroom. It seeps into the very fabric of how societies perceive justice, leading to erosion in public trust. When citizens can't distinguish truth from fabrication, faith in legal institutions wanes, creating a pervasive cynicism. It's a scenario ripe for exploitation, where certain entities leverage misinformation to undermine opponents or sway public discourse. This is a profound concern as eroded trust in justice systems can destabilize not just individual cases but the broader societal contract of law and order.

Consider the unique complexities misinformation introduces into legal procedures: the need for new vetting mechanisms, technologies to discern fact from falsehood, and policies to address the rapid spread of inaccuracies. Lawyers and judges must now be part digital detectives, capable of navigating through a morass of data, identifying credible sources, and discarding the rest. Legal education must also evolve, incorporating new methodologies to prepare future practitioners for this landscape fraught with informational pitfalls.

So what's the remedy in a world that seems to churn out misinformation at an alarming rate? Strengthening the resilience of our justice systems against misinformation requires actionable strategies. Collaborative efforts between tech companies, legal entities, and educational institutions can innovate solutions to verify facts swiftly and accurately. Moreover, cultivating a culture of critical thinking among the populace can arm society against the onslaught of falsehoods. In this way, truth can reclaim its rightful place at the heart of justice, and our evolving systems can continue their quest to uphold it.

In closing, safeguarding the sanctity of truth in our legal systems amidst a sea of misinformation is not merely a challenge but a necessity. If left unchecked, this harbinger of falsehoods threatens to unravel the very principles of justice that bind our societies together. In tackling misinformation head-on, we not only preserve the integrity of our legal frameworks but also renew our commitment to the truth, ensuring it prevails in the ever-changing face of justice. The stakes couldn't be higher, yet the potential rewards—the restoration of trust and confidence in our legal institutions—are well worth the effort.

The Challenge of Verifying Facts

In today's rapidly evolving world, verifying facts is no longer a straightforward endeavor, especially within the intricate labyrinth of legal systems. What was once a relatively modest task of examining evidence and attesting to its truth has now burgeoned into an elaborate challenge, rife with complexity and peril. Why, you might ask? Because we're living in an age where misinformation flows as freely as water, and the truth is often obscured under layers of half-truths and deliberate fabrications.

The decline of veracity in legal systems isn't accidental. It's a confluence of technological advancements and societal shifts that has led to a landscape where the line between what's real and what's not is constantly blurred. Lawyers, judges, and jurors now face the monumental task of navigating through this labyrinth, armed only with tools that aren't always equipped to deal with the digital age's demands. Consider the scenario where digital records, supposedly concrete sources of truth, can be manipulated with nothing more than a few keystrokes. In this environment, how can one confidently assert the authenticity of evidence?

The information age has opened a Pandora's box of sorts. The floodgates of information, once tightly controlled, have been unleashed. Data is everywhere, yet this glut doesn't equate to clarity. On the contrary, it muddies the waters, making discernment not only difficult but in some cases, nearly impossible. Legal professionals must now parse through overwhelming volumes of data, using critical analysis not just to find what is pertinent, but to ascertain its accuracy and intent. This problem is further exacerbated when considering the pace of information dissemination, often far outstripping the ability of legal systems to efficiently scrutinize and verify.

We've all seen how a single erroneous piece of information, a deceptive photograph, or an insidious video can spread like wildfire, ensnaring the unwary and misinforming the masses. These dynamics are doubly challenging in a courtroom setting, where the stakes are often nothing less than life and liberty. Furthermore, as facts become contentious battlegrounds, legal systems experience strains similar to those faced by public discourse, where once seemingly stable definitions of truth are questioned and redefined.

The enormity of this challenge calls into question the very frameworks upon which justice is built. Concepts such as "beyond a reasonable doubt" take on new meanings when facing facts that require Herculean efforts just to substantiate. Moreover, as technology continues to integrate into every facet of life, our strategies for evaluating facts must adapt as well. This means not only judicial reforms but also innovative approaches within legal education and practice, equipping future generations to handle these unprecedented challenges.

Yet, the attempt to verify facts is not solely an institutional burden. It raises broader philosophical questions about the nature of truth and the role of legal systems in safeguarding it. Ideally, the law acts as a bulwark against deception, ensuring that justice is served based on a foundation of verifiable reality. But when the reliability of facts is undermined, can justice truly be said to prevail? This dilemma doesn't just haunt the courtrooms but touches the core of societal trust and cohesion.

There is, of course, hope on the horizon. Technological solutions like blockchain, touted for its incorruptibility, are being explored for secure record-keeping. Likewise, advances in artificial intelligence present opportunities for scrutinizing data with heightened precision and accuracy. Yet, such tools must be wielded with care, for while they promise much, they can also carry risks if not judiciously applied. This interplay between technology and veracity requires not just technical acumen but ethical clarity from those guiding the evolution of legal systems.

In wrestling with the challenge of verifying facts, the legal community must embark on a renaissance of sorts, drawing from philosophy, technology, and human insight. It must evolve, not just react, to this era's demands, crafting strategies that transcend traditional methods of evidence evaluation. The truth, it seems, is not a destination but an ongoing journey, one that demands continual reevaluation and recalibration in the face of new challenges and possibilities.

The stakes couldn't be higher. Inadequate mechanisms for fact verification threaten to erode the very legitimacy of legal systems. Conflicts over truth have repercussions that ripple far beyond the courtroom, influencing public perception and impacting global justice efforts. This battle for truth is not limited by borders or jurisdictions but is a universal challenge that calls for collective resolve and inventive solutions from all corners of the legal world.

Ultimately, the resilience of legal systems hinges on their ability to adapt and confront these challenges head-on, for in the face of uncertainty, a steadfast commitment to truth becomes the ultimate ally. Only by doing so can they maintain their sacred mandate to uphold justice and protect the rights of every individual, even in an age where facts are as contested as the laws that seek to govern them.

Chapter 4:
Justice and Public Perception

The courtroom, once a revered place for the search for truth, now finds itself sharing the stage with the court of public opinion. The latter, fueled by the rapid-fire narratives of social media and the relentless 24-hour news cycle, exerts a poignant influence on how justice is perceived in society today. It's a complex dance where reality and perception often get tangled, resulting in a delicate balance that legal systems worldwide struggle to maintain.

Public perception of justice isn't just a backdrop; it's a powerful driver that can bolster or erode the credibility of legal institutions. Perceptions, unlike objective truths, don't necessarily require evidence. They thrive on impressions, stories, and the overarching societal narratives that individuals and communities hold dear. It's here that the media plays a starring role, shaping, reshaping, and sometimes distorting these perceptions. In some instances, sensationalized reporting oversimplifies complex legal proceedings, leading to misconceptions that shake the public's faith in justice systems.

Contrast this with the core principle of justice: the belief in fairness, impartiality, and due process. Today, despite extensive coverage, many individuals feel distant from these pillars, primarily because the narratives they consume often emphasize cases where justice appears to fail. This distortion leads to a pervasive skepticism. Can justice truly be fair when the stories in the headlines suggest otherwise?

The relationship between justice and public perception is not a unidirectional flow but rather an intricate web of influence. On one hand, justice outcomes shape public opinion; on the other, public opinion pressures the system to act in certain ways. When the public loses trust, the legitimacy of legal institutions falters, triggering a vicious cycle of doubt and delegitimization. Policymakers and scholars need to be acutely aware of this interaction, as it can determine whether legal systems are seen as bastions of fairness or relics of a bygone era.

Yet, it's not just about media influence. The pervasive decline in public trust ties deeply into broader social phenomena. Increasing polarization, fueled by echo chambers and ideological silos, creates environments where like-minded individuals reinforce each other's beliefs, often without question. Justice becomes less about impartiality and more about "us" versus "them."

This erosion of trust presents a substantial challenge, particularly in democratic societies that depend on the public's belief in the rule of law. When confidence wanes, there are real-world consequences—not just in courtroom decisions but in compliance with laws themselves. Citizens may start to question not only the outcomes of high-profile cases but their very foundations. Are laws applied equally? Does money or influence buy a different brand of justice? Such questions linger ominously in the public consciousness, eroding the bedrock of trust upon which societies function.

Moreover, this atmosphere of doubt places an enormous burden on legal practitioners, who may feel caught between staying true to legal principles and responding to the clamor of public opinion. It's a tightrope walk, where the impartial must sometimes become the advocate—defending the virtue of a system perceived to be faltering.

Reinvigorating public trust requires more than mere reassurances. It demands comprehensive strategies, from increased transparency in legal proceedings to fostering greater public understanding of how justice is dispensed. Policymakers must champion reforms that bridge the gap between perception and reality, presenting law not as an arcane discipline but as a dynamic process open to scrutiny and evolution.

Transparency isn't merely about opening the courtroom doors wider but also about engaging in honest conversations about justice's aspirations and its limitations. Educating the public becomes crucial, not in broad strokes, but with nuanced discussions about how cases are adjudicated, the role of evidence, and the complexities of law interpretation.

In this endeavor, partnerships with media organizations can prove invaluable. Encouraging responsible reporting and providing training for journalists to cover legal matters objectively can be significant steps forward. Journalists and legal experts must collaborate to ensure that what's reported not only informs but also educates, providing context that tempers raw reactions.

Meanwhile, there's an urgent call for legal systems themselves to be more adaptable. Moving with the times doesn't mean compromising on foundational principles but rather embracing innovations that modernize procedures, making them more relatable to the public. For instance, incorporating digital platforms to demystify legal processes or leveraging technology to enhance public access to legal documents can increase transparency and trust.

Understanding justice and public perception's nuanced relationship can lead us to actionable insights. With this awareness, legal scholars, policymakers, and concerned citizens are better equipped to navigate the turbulent waters where public perception meets legal reality. Justice should not only be done but also be seen to be done, resonating with clarity and fairness across all strata of society.

The Media's Role in Shaping Perceptions...In an age where information is both abundant and complex, the media plays a crucial role in shaping public perception of justice. For many, the media acts as the first and most frequent lens through which the notion of justice is viewed. This positioning carries with it a significant responsibility but also layers of challenges, particularly when it comes to the verification of facts. The reputation of legal institutions, the nuances of court decisions, and the portrayal of justice-related issues all heavily rely on the media's interpretation and dissemination.

The power of media lies in its ability to reach millions instantly. However, with this power comes an equally potent capacity to distort, whether intentionally or inadvertently. News outlets often grapple with deadlines and the race for viewership, sometimes prioritizing speed over accuracy. The pursuit for immediacy can lead to oversimplification of complex legal matters or misrepresentation of facts. This misalignment not only undermines public trust but also fuels the spread of misinformation, intertwining it deeply with the challenge of verifying facts in a fast-paced media environment. Excellence breeds expectation, and when the media misses the mark, public perceptions of justice suffer.

Moreover, the fragmentation of media into echo chambers complicates the landscape further. In today's world, individuals are more likely to seek information from sources that affirm their existing beliefs, creating a skewed perception of justice. This phenomenon, known as confirmation bias, amplifies the divide between objective legal realities and subjective public opinions. The challenge grows as the line between factual reporting and opinion becomes increasingly blurred.

The proliferation of social media adds another complex layer. Platforms like Twitter and Facebook serve not only as channels for news dissemination but also as breeding grounds for hurried judgments and viral misinformation. A snippet, tweet, or headline can incite widespread reactions before the full story even unfolds, leaving legal truths in its wake. Here lies the media's delicate task: to present verifiable facts clearly while acknowledging the speed and reach of the digital information age.

While enduring these trials, the media also retains the potential to enlighten and educate. It can be an instrumental tool in demystifying legal processes and enhancing public understanding of justice. By engaging with experts, providing context, and prioritizing accuracy over sensationalism, the media can transform from a source of confusion to a beacon of clarity. This transformative role reinforces the pressing need for journalistic standards that reflect depth, integrity, and adherence to truth.

If the media can consistently uphold these standards, it stands capable of recalibrating public trust in legal systems. It can bridge the gap between the abstract intricacies of justice and the tangible perceptions of everyday citizens. The key lies in rediscovering its role as not just a broadcaster of news but a curator of truth. In doing so, the media becomes an integral component in the quest for a more just society, where facts triumph over fiction.

Public Trust in Legal Institutions When it comes to justice, securing public trust in our legal institutions is absolutely essential. Yet, in contemporary society, we find ourselves grappling with "The Challenge of Verifying Facts", an issue that profoundly impacts this trust. Inaccurate information can spread like wildfire, thanks to the internet and social media. Consequently, the legal system, traditionally seen as the bastion of truth, is perceived as faltering under these new pressures.

Imagine being on a jury, inundated with conflicting facts. How are ordinary citizens expected to discern truth from fiction when even seasoned legal experts struggle? This is where public trust is tested the most. If legal institutions are going to maintain or regain public confidence, they need robust mechanisms for fact verification, which involve transparency and clarity in how they operate. The consequences of failing to address this challenge are dire, potentially leading to a populace that questions the very foundation of justice.

So, what can be done? It starts with acknowledging the problem and committing to solutions that embrace technological advancements without compromising the principles of justice. For example, the marriage of rigorous fact-checking protocols with transparent communication can help bridge this trust gap. By demystifying legal proceedings and embracing a culture of openness, legal institutions can invariably fortify their credibility. All stakeholders—concerned citizens, legal scholars, policymakers—must unite in reinforcing this trust. The stakes are far too high for complacency.

Chapter 5:
International Perspectives on Justice

Justice, a concept so often taken for granted, varies greatly around the globe. It's easy to assume that what works for one nation will naturally work for another. Yet, as we peel back the layers of legal systems worldwide, we find a tapestry woven with threads of different histories, cultures, and socio-political landscapes. In this chapter, "International Perspectives on Justice," we explore the diverse ways societies define and administer justice, revealing both surprising contrasts and unexpected similarities.

Consider the differences between common law countries like the United States and the United Kingdom, and civil law countries such as France and Germany. These systems, rooted in unique historical contexts, shape how justice is perceived and executed. In common law jurisdictions, the emphasis lies heavily on judicial precedents and the interpretative power of court decisions. In contrast, civil law systems prioritize codified statutes over judicial rulings. This fundamental difference often leads to varied approaches in addressing legal challenges.

Let's look at Asia, an expanse of legal traditions as wide as its physical dimensions. In Japan, the system blends elements of civil law with customary practices, heavily emphasizing reconciliation and social harmony. Meanwhile, in India, the legal landscape is a complex interplay of colonial legacies, religious laws, and various amendments intended to address modern societal changes. Such diversity illustrates differing priorities—Japan aims for societal peace, whereas India grapples with accommodating a vast, pluralistic society.

However, international justice also involves navigating the challenges posed by globalization. Borders are no longer barriers to issues like cybercrime, human trafficking, and environmental damage. As a result, countries are increasingly interdependent in their quest for justice. Institutions like the International Criminal Court and various human rights councils strive to bridge this gap, although their efficacy is often a subject of debate. Who gets to decide what's just and unjust on an international scale?

Turning our gaze to Latin America—where many countries have struggled with authoritarianism and political corruption—a recurring theme is the resistance against these influences. Legal systems in this region often reflect the tension between maintaining rule of law and addressing human rights violations. Nations like Chile and Argentina have made noteworthy strides in reforming their judicial processes post-dictatorship, yet challenges persist in terms of ensuring judicial independence and integrity.

Africa's justice systems are equally diverse, reflecting its colonial past, indigenous laws, and modern statehood. Countries like South Africa have been lauded for constructing a system that incorporates strong constitutional mandates protecting all citizens' rights. Meanwhile, regions facing instability and conflict, such as the Democratic Republic of the Congo, often suffer from a breakdown in legal order, underscoring how fragile justice systems can be under duress.

Across Europe, the European Union attempts to foster legal harmony among member states. It's a continual balancing act as nations strive to maintain individuality while adhering to EU directives aimed at ensuring cohesive justice. Initiatives like the European Convention on Human Rights demonstrate how continental efforts work towards upholding shared values, although compliance remains uneven among countries.

In examining international perspectives on justice, it's critical not to overlook the role of culture and tradition. Customary laws still hold sway in many regions, coexisting with modern legal practices. This duality can sometimes create friction, where traditional norms conflict with national laws or international human rights standards. Yet, in other cases, they complement each other, evolving to better serve contemporary societies.

These international perspectives underscore a crucial point: a one-size-fits-all approach to justice is neither feasible nor desirable. Each system contains lessons that can inform others, even as each must address its own unique challenges. The interconnected nature of our world means that what happens in one corner can ripple across to another, necessitating dialogue and collaboration over rigid replication of legal systems.

As we advance in this book, let's keep these global insights in mind. They highlight not only the disparities but also the shared aspirations towards achieving justice. It takes continual effort to foster systems that truly serve their people, and the evolution of global justice is an endeavor that requires collective attention and action.

Comparative Analysis of Global Systems explores a topic that couldn't be more pertinent today: the challenge of verifying facts in an interconnected world where justice no longer has singular interpretations. Across the globe, leaders and citizens alike grapple with legal systems that, while structured around universal legal principles, diverge wildly in their methods of fact verification.

In nations where legal traditions are steeped in adversarial systems, the pursuit of truth sometimes takes a backseat to the tactics of winning cases. Contrast this with inquisitorial systems, where judges play an active role in investigating cases and seeking factual truths. Each system, though fundamentally different, is now facing a common enemy—misinformation. The rapid spread of distorted data across digital platforms is not limited by borders, making the verification of facts a universal conundrum.

Consider the approach to digital evidence, a burgeoning area of concern. Western nations such as the United States grapple with the sheer volume of data, requiring sophisticated algorithms and new legal standards to ascertain reliability. On the other hand, countries in regions such as the European Union have implemented stricter data protection regulations, which complicate the straightforward use of digital evidence in courtrooms. This divergence highlights a critical issue: while the challenge of verifying facts is universal, the solutions are not one-size-fits-all.

In juxtaposing these systems, it's evident that justice is not a monolith. The truth remains as elusive as ever, slipping through the fingers of legal entities trying to capture its essence amidst waves of misinformation. Countries that once held the belief that their system of justice was impervious now realize that without accurate fact-verification mechanisms, credibility falters, and trust erodes.

Furthermore, cultural dimensions impact how different societies tackle these obstacles. In some Eastern nations, communal consensus plays a significant role in the pursuit of justice, emphasizing societal harmony over individual legal battles. This communal aspect can affect how facts are verified and accepted, posing questions about the balance between societal norms and legal standards.

In this swirling mix of practices and challenges, international collaborations become not just beneficial but essential. Legal scholars and policymakers find themselves at a crossroads, tasked with the arduous yet critical mission of harmonizing these disparate systems.

The goal? To devise globally coherent strategies that uphold justice while respecting cultural and systemic diversity.

As we navigate through this chapter on international perspectives, it becomes clear that the task at hand is as formidable as it is pressing. Solutions must be innovative, built on mutual understanding, and committed to maintaining the sanctity of truth across borders. In doing so, we hope to bolster global justice systems against the tides of misinformation. The future of global legal integrity hinges on it.

Case Studies of Erosion often serve as a mirror reflecting the profound challenges within the section, "The Challenge of Verifying Facts." In today's fast-paced world, where information crosses borders at the speed of a click, ensuring the veracity of statements in international legal contexts has become more daunting than ever. As courts and legal systems grapple with misinformation and the erosion of truth, examining these case studies provides crucial insights into how justice can sometimes falter.

In one notable case, the rapid spread of falsified news reports significantly influenced the outcome of judicial proceedings in a European country. Here, the influx of doctored evidence disseminated through digital channels led to public uproar and misguided judicial pressure. The erosion of fact became apparent when legal counsel, deeply reliant on publicly accessible data, found themselves ensnared in a web of falsehoods. It's a chilling reminder of how easily justice can be manipulated, illustrating the urgent need for stringent mechanisms to authenticate evidence and safeguard judicial integrity.

Across the Atlantic, a different scenario unfolded with similar undertones of erosion. In the context of political upheaval, a prominent South American nation witnessed the politicization of its judicial system, leading to a crisis of trust. Here, misinformation wasn't just a side act; it played a starring role, casting doubt on established legal principles and contributing to the miscarriage of justice. The state's failure to verify dubious claims undermined public confidence and called into question the impartiality of its legal processes. This case underscores how erosion isn't merely an abstract concept but a real-world challenge demanding attention and action.

In the legal labyrinth of another judicial system, the complexity of cross-border litigation highlighted another layer of erosion. Distorted facts and discrepancies in the authentication of international documents led to unexpected legal delays and unwarranted decisions. The difficulty in verifying facts across jurisdictions exposed vulnerabilities in international cooperation, demonstrating how easy it is for erosion to creep in and complicate the already intricate weave of global justice systems. Such case studies are more than just cautionary tales; they're calls to action for bolstering international legal standards and technology to preserve truth.

The lessons drawn from these case studies aren't just academic—they're a clarion call for policymakers and scholars alike. What's clear is the necessity to bolster existing frameworks that can better address these challenges. But beyond systemic reforms, there's a need for a cultural shift towards valuing truth, accuracy, and integrity in our information ecosystems. Such shifts ensure that justice isn't just eroded by falsehoods but is continually reinforced by the diligent pursuit of truth. It's time we acknowledge these crackling fissures and fortify our commitment to justice around the globe.

Chapter 6:
Technology's Impact on
Legal Precedent

Technology, a relentless force in modern society, has fundamentally reshaped countless aspects of our lives. From how we communicate to how we work, its fingerprints are everywhere. Yet perhaps nowhere is this influence more contentious and consequential than in the realm of legal precedent. Legal systems, traditionally glued to bookshelves weighed down by massive tomes, are being propelled into the digital age at breakneck speed. This transition brings with it a slew of challenges and opportunities—a legal frontier marked by digital evidence and artificial intelligence.

The rise of digital evidence marks a significant departure from traditional forms of proof. Gone are the days when paper trails dominated courtrooms. Instead, emails, text messages, and other forms of digital communication have started to take center stage. They provide real-time records but open a can of worms concerning authenticity and privacy. How do we ensure an email isn't fabricated? Who verifies the chain of custody for a series of text messages?

These questions are not merely hypothetical. Increasingly, courts must confront the reality that digital evidence can be manipulated with alarming ease. Software exists that can alter digital files without any trace of tampering, posing unprecedented challenges to legal integrity. Judges and juries, often not digital natives, face the daunting task of separating fact from fiction armed with nothing more than layperson understandings of complex technologies.

Layered on top of these challenges is the role of artificial intelligence in courts. AI tools promise a future where routine legal processes become more efficient, potentially saving time and resources. Sorting through mountains of documents for discovery becomes a task not for humans, but for algorithms. AI has already been used to predict judicial outcomes, ostensibly making the legal system predictably rational—but is it truly rational, or does it reinforce existing biases?

The ethical implications of AI in legal proceedings are profound. Consider sentencing algorithms that predict recidivism: they offer a veneer of scientific objectivity but often reflect systemic prejudices embedded in historical data. The specter of biased algorithms making life-altering decisions on behalf of judges is more than a theoretical fear—it's an observable reality. The technology was meant to democratize, but what if it perpetuates inequalities instead?

Furthermore, the role of AI raises another crucial issue: transparency. A judge's decision can be scrutinized, but an algorithm's inner workings often remain a black box. This opacity poses a dire threat to legal accountability. If we don't know why an AI made a particular decision, how can we ensure justice has truly been served?

Another critical concern is the regulatory framework—or lack thereof—governing the use of technology in legal systems. As technology evolves, existing laws often lag, leaving gaping holes in oversight and accountability. Policymakers are scrambling to develop legal parameters that appropriately address the fast-paced advancements in technology, yet their efforts are frequently reactive rather than proactive. It's a game of perpetual catch-up that risks eroding public trust.

Consider, too, the global dimension of these challenges. The influence of technology knows no borders, yet legal systems are inextricably tied to national governance. This dynamic creates a complex web where technology's impact must be navigated differently across jurisdictions, often leading to fragmented and inconsistent practices. Are we facing a future where justice is not universal but instead determined by the capacity of a legal system to keep up technologically?

Despite these hurdles, technology's potential to enhance justice cannot be entirely overshadowed by its pitfalls. Properly harnessed, digital tools can democratize access to legal resources. Imagine virtual courtrooms where geographic barriers dissolve and legal representation becomes more accessible for countless individuals. Or consider crowdsourced platforms that offer legal advice, bridging the information gap for those who'd otherwise be in the dark.

For the legal scholars, policymakers, and concerned citizens examining these issues, the path forward demands a multifaceted approach. Education and awareness are alchemy in this landscape. Training legal practitioners to not only adopt but critically engage with technology is a crucial first step. Robust regulatory frameworks need to be established, scientists and technologists must be collaborators, not mere bystanders, in this process.

By raising awareness and prompting action, we can steer technology's trajectory in law toward a future where it amplifies justice rather than warping it. The dialogue between technology and law is ongoing, a narrative with the power to redefine societal norms. It is both an exciting and daunting prospect, laden with the potential to radically reshape the world as we know it. The onus is on us, in the here and now, to ensure that this narrative is one we can be proud to tell to future generations.

Digital Evidence and Its Challenges is a sub-section under the broader exploration of how technology is reshaping legal precedent in the modern age. Today, we're faced with a paradox. Digital evidence, including everything from text messages to videos, offers a bounty of information for legal proceedings. Yet, it simultaneously complicates the already Herculean task of verifying facts. As technology intertwines itself more deeply into our daily lives, it creates a dense web; navigating it is both an opportunity and a challenge for the law.

Think about it: in the age of smartphones and ubiquitous surveillance, crucial evidence can be gathered in an instant. A few taps and swipes can preserve events that might have otherwise slipped into the ether. But herein lies the rub: digital data is inherently malleable. It's surprisingly easy to manipulate or distort. Photoshop can alter images, deepfakes can fabricate video, and edited audio tracks can insert words that were never uttered. So, how can the legal systems, steeped in centuries-old traditions of justice and fact-finding, adapt to this morphing landscape?

A powerful, undeniable image or a series of text messages can make or break a case, which emphasizes the importance of authenticity. Yet, with the ease of fabrication, lawyers and judges have to ask themselves: Is what they see real? Traditional methods of evidence verification, relying heavily on eyewitnesses, don't always translate neatly into the digital realm. Digital trails can be misleading, and the risk of misinterpretation skyrockets when algorithms, not humans, play judge and jury.

Moreover, the tech-savvy individual can easily erase or modify information. In certain cases, entire digital histories can mysteriously vanish. You're left with a gaping hole where your evidence ought to be. This malleability imparts a certain ephemerality to digital evidence, one that's at odds with the permanence typically required in legal investigations. The law must figure out a way to differentiate between data tampering and genuine artifacts, an unenviable task given the complexity involved.

And what about security? Here we have another layer of complexity. Cybersecurity experts play a crucial role in safeguarding digital evidence from tampering. They fortify digital files with encryption and authenticity seals, like the digital signatures that serve as the gold standard for unaltered data. However, even these can sometimes be compromised. In the cat-and-mouse game of digital forensics, what's secure today might be vulnerable tomorrow.

Compounding these problems is the fact that legal professionals may not possess adequate technological literacy to effectively navigate these challenges. This skills gap can lead to oversights, with potentially dire consequences for justice. Courts are grappling with how to handle such fast-evolving forms of evidence. The need for specialized training programs to better equip legal teams and judges is urgent. Without it, the risk of wrongful convictions or acquittals based merely on manipulated evidence remains disturbingly real.

In conclusion, digital evidence stands as a testament to both the relentless march of technological progress and its knotty challenges. Our fiduciary responsibility is unmistakable: build legal frameworks robust enough to incorporate technical advancements without sacrificing the integrity of truth. Lawmakers, judges, legal experts, and technologists must work in concert to transform these digital complexities into well-understood, manageable paradigms. Only then can we hope to keep justice as anchored and steadfast as society needs it to be.

The Role of Artificial Intelligence in Courts advances our chapter about technology's impact on legal precedent. In the ever-complicated world of law, the question isn't whether artificial intelligence (AI) will influence courtrooms, but how it will change the dynamics of truth and fact-verification. The courts, despite their established traditions and adherence to history, are not immune to such sweeping technological transformations. The challenge of verifying facts, one of the legal sector's oldest conundrums, takes on an entirely new dimension with AI, presenting both hope and a labyrinth of potential pitfalls.

AI's most promising role in courtrooms centers around enhancing the accuracy and speed of fact-checking. Legal systems often buckle under immense data-heavy cases, where the sheer volume of evidence can be overwhelming. AI can sift through mountains of documents, presenting verified information efficiently and accurately. This means courts could theoretically reduce time spent in deliberation, allowing for a more streamlined judicial process. Yet, real concerns persist: how do we ensure the integrity of the algorithms? Are they really neutral, or do we inadvertently program our biases into them?

One of AI's significant advantages in legal settings is its ability to discern patterns that humans might miss. In cases where historical data might illuminate behavior or suggest motives, AI's pattern recognition faculties can be invaluable. Consider complex financial fraud cases where AI tools can follow money trails with precision, something human analysts might take years to comprehend fully. However, reliance on AI is not a cure-all; it requires judicious application complemented by the discerning eye of a seasoned legal mind.

However, the reliance on AI for fact verification raises essential questions about transparency and accountability. Can judges and juries, responsible for determining truth and justice, comprehend the methodologies behind AI's conclusions? Ensuring that AI's processes are transparent and understandable is crucial not just for judicial trust but for public confidence as well. After all, a black box algorithm can't replace the critical thinking we've long associated with human decision-makers.

Moreover, deploying AI in courtrooms creates practical and ethical dilemmas. On the one hand, it amplifies our capacity to manage data and verify facts more effectively, making justice theoretically more attainable. On the other hand, legal practitioners must grapple with issues of privacy, consent, and the risk of over-reliance. If an AI algorithm commits an error, who bears responsibility? Do we pass the judgment onto the creators, the regulators, or the court that used it?

In this context, AI is not just a tool but also a potential reformer of the very principles that underpin our legal systems. The implications of AI's role in courtrooms extend far beyond efficiency gains—they strike at the heart of what we consider just and equitable in the legal process. As we embrace AI's potential, we must also maintain a critical eye on its limitations and ensure that our legal systems evolve thoughtfully, preserving the core tenets of justice while integrating innovations that serve the greater good.

Chapter 7:
Political Influence on Legal Integrity

The entanglement of politics and the legal system has long been both a delicate dance and a troubling specter in the halls of justice. In contemporary society, this intersection looms larger, threatening the integrity of the systems designed to uphold law and order. *Political Influence on Legal Integrity* is a discourse becoming increasingly relevant as callous manipulations threaten the very tenets of fairness and impartiality within legal institutions. This interplay, where political agendas encroach upon judicial processes, demands our scrutiny.

Politicians often wield substantial power to steer legal outcomes, whether through the appointment of judges, drafting of laws, or prioritizing certain cases over others. Consider the appointment process. Here, ideological preferences take precedence, compromising the pose of a neutral judiciary committed to justice over partisanship. Judges who are expected to be bastions of morality are sometimes chosen for their political alignments rather than their judicial merits. Once revered as symbols of objectivity, courts are increasingly perceived as battlegrounds for political warfare.

Moreover, legislative bodies frequently pass laws that do not just reflect societal norms but cater to political interests. These laws might benefit specific groups or further the agendas of those in power, leaving marginalized communities in a legal limbo. Such actions not only contravene the principle of equity but also plant seeds of distrust in the legal framework. When laws and policies become tools for political maneuvering, they inherently weaken the structural foundation they are supposed to fortify.

Our globalized world offers numerous examples of political interference in legal systems. From overt actions like the dismissal of impartial judges under authoritarian regimes, to subtler tactics such as manipulating public perception through media, the misuse of political power is widespread. Each incident chips away at the judiciary's credibility, eroding public confidence and fostering a climate of cynicism. In this charged environment, the concept of "justice for all" risks becoming a hollow proclamation.

Political influence is not sole in the appointments and laws; it also infiltrates the prosecutorial processes. Public prosecutors, often subject to election processes or political oversight, might prioritize cases that offer political capital or shield political allies from scrutiny. This approach converts legal pursuits into mere political theater, diverting resources away from cases of genuine public concern. The spectacle sacrifices the ideals of justice to the whims of political strategy.

In navigating these challenging waters, nations must prioritize strengthening the independence of their judicial systems. This includes fostering environments where legal interpretations are guided by fact and fairness rather than political expediency. Safeguards should be enacted to shield judicial appointments from partisan influence, allowing meritocracy and integrity to stand as deciding factors for judicial candidates.

Another line of defense lies in cultivating a well-informed citizenry. People who understand the mechanics of their legal institutions can better hold government accountable. This knowledge arms them against the narrative spins of political actors who may seek to undermine judicial autonomy for their advantage. Civic education and public engagement stand as pillars to counterbalance political overreach.

The confluence of politics and law is, in essence, neither inherently negative nor positive. It is a natural occurrence in societies where governance and jurisprudence overlap. Yet, without vigilant checks and balances, this interplay threatens to distort the legal landscape beyond repair. It calls for actions that promote transparency, uphold ethical standards, and most importantly—embody an unwavering commitment to justice as a universal principle, free from the contaminating touch of political ambition.

Ultimately, the responsibility to preserve legal integrity lies not only with the judiciary or politicians but with all of us—citizens, scholars, policymakers alike. By fostering institutions that are resilient to political tides, and by demanding adherence to the rule of law over rule by law, we can ensure that justice remains untainted, standing steadfast as the cornerstone of civil society.

The Intersection of Law and Politics presents a nuanced frontier where truth is often contested, especially when it comes to verifying facts. It's a battleground that challenges the very bedrock of legal integrity. In today's landscape, politics doesn't merely influence law; it saturates it. The tension between objective legal principles and political motivations can often muddy the waters of justice, leaving citizens, scholars, and policymakers grappling with the implications.

Political influence can distort fact-finding missions, akin to adding fog to already murky waters. It's not enough to have established facts; the interpretation and presentation of these truths are equally crucial. When political aims creep into the judicial system, the quest for clear, factual verification becomes entangled in a web of bias and spin. The challenge, then, is to discern facts from fabrications and motivations from merit, ensuring that legal processes remain a bastion of integrity even amidst political noise.

This intersection calls for vigilant oversight and an unwavering commitment to truth. The law strives to hold steady as a neutral entity, yet its stewards must navigate the political terrain, often walking a tightrope between impartiality and influence. As citizens, scholars, or policymakers, understanding these dynamics is essential. It means advocating for transparency and demanding accountability at every twist and turn of legal proceedings. By fortifying the legal system against political erosion, we aim to safeguard the fundamental principles that underpin justice itself.

Case Studies of Political Interference In examining the intricate dance between politics and the justice system, several case studies vividly illustrate the challenge of verifying facts. Political interference often muddies the waters of truth, leaving justice systems groping in the dark. Let's start with a memorable instance from a country where democracy was believed to be well-established: the judicial appointments scandal. Here, political leverage was wielded with precision, resulting in the nomination and appointment of judges aligned not by merit but by political allegiance. The integrity of these appointments was defended with fervor, yet whispers of collusion never quite died down. Notably, when court decisions appeared to follow political lines, the public trust took a significant hit.

Another case worthy of scrutiny involved the suppression of evidence deemed politically sensitive. Reports emerged suggesting that a high-profile corruption investigation was halted midstream due to pressure from influential political figures. Those in power deployed clever tactics—shifting narratives and complex legal jargon—to obscure the truth. Verifying the precise facts of this interference proved nearly impossible, as investigative avenues were blocked or dismantled, leaving the public in a spiral of doubt and distrust. The arm-wrestling for control over what constitutes admissible evidence becomes even more of a challenge when facts are seen as malleable tools rather than immovable truths.

Now consider a government heavily influenced by the need to secure electoral victory. In this scenario, legal systems were manipulated through the promulgation of ordinances that favored the ruling party's supporters. On paper, these legal changes seemed innocuous, yet beneath the surface lay a calculated attempt to tilt the democratic scale. Again, verifying these under-the-table maneuvers was daunting, exacerbated by a lack of transparency. Legal scholars found themselves grappling with interpretations that skewed the law's original intent, illustrating the ways in which political interference can reshape legal landscapes and erode justice.

Let's not forget international examples, which reflect similar challenges. In a geopolitical hotspot, political leaders sought to influence the judiciary's independence by financially constraining its operations. The cuts were disguised as budgetary necessities, yet they functioned as a strategic assault on a justice system attempting to operate free from the shadows of political puppeteers. In this context, discerning the real from the fabricated was like peeling a seemingly infinite onion, each layer more pungent than the last.

These case studies serve as a wake-up call. As political interests entwine with legal mandates, the very sanctity of what is deemed factual comes into question. Without rigorous fact verification, we risk witnessing further erosion of legal integrity worldwide. The onus, therefore, is on concerned citizens, legal scholars, and policymakers alike to advocate for and implement robust mechanisms that anchor our justice systems firmly to undeniable truths. Political interference may seem like an unstoppable tide, yet with diligence and collective will, maintaining transparency and truth remains a reachable goal.

Chapter 8:
Social Inequality and Legal Systems

As we dive into the complexities of social inequality and legal systems, it becomes painfully clear that the scales of justice are not as balanced as we'd like to believe. The intersection of socioeconomic status and access to legal recourse reveals disparities that are neither new nor insignificant. From courtrooms that echo with biases to legal costs that act as barriers, the system often acts unequally, perpetuating cycles of disadvantage for the underprivileged.

Consider this: the right to an attorney, a cornerstone of democratic justice, is rendered almost meaningless for those unable to afford adequate representation. Public defenders are often overwhelmed, juggling an untenable number of cases, which leaves them with little time or resources to mount a robust defense. As a result, the quality of legal defense a person receives is often directly proportional to their financial means. This stark reality prompts an essential question—how can justice prevail when it's contingent on one's socioeconomic standing rather than the merit of one's case?

The situation is further exacerbated by the lack of legal resources available to marginalized communities. Legal aid organizations strive to fill the gap, but they are frequently underfunded and overstretched. This forces them to prioritize cases, often leaving many without the help they desperately need. It's a grim paradox that while the law is designed to be blind, the system enforcing it frequently sees in shades tinted by wealth and privilege.

Unequal access to justice isn't just a domestic problem; it's a global issue that paints with broad strokes across different societies and legal systems. In many parts of the world, systemic discrimination rooted in ethnicity, gender, or age further complicates access to justice. This global perspective challenges us to think beyond our own legal frameworks and consider the universal principles that should guide equitable legal systems.

Moreover, the legal landscape is riddled with rules and procedures that can be incredibly confusing to those without specialized knowledge. Socioeconomic disparities exacerbate this confusion, as individuals with limited education may struggle even more to navigate the legal maze. For them, a courtroom can feel as foreign as a different country, underscoring the critical need for legal systems that are accessible and understandable.

Efforts to address these inequities aren't absent, but they need to be intensified. Advocacy for systemic changes, such as reformed bail systems and equitable legal representation, remains crucial. Legal systems must be reimagined to serve all citizens equitably, regardless of their social and economic background. Policymakers have a responsibility to act, transforming aspiring ideals into living realities.

The rhetoric surrounding law and order frequently overlooks the quiet inequities simmering underneath the surface. When laws disproportionately impact lower-income individuals or minority communities, the promise of justice is but a hollow echo. It's incumbent upon us to question, to challenge, and ultimately, to dismantle the fragile veneers that superficially paint our systems as just.

In this quest, dialogue and awareness play pivotal roles. Engaging discussions that bring these issues to light can spark change. It's also important to leverage the power of education and information to bridge the gap between the public and the legal system, ensuring that justice is not merely a privilege of the well-heeled.

Rooted in historical injustices, today's legal inequalities are intertwined with a past that must be acknowledged and addressed. Understanding the complex web of socio-legal dynamics is not an academic exercise but a moral imperative that beckons action. The work to rectify these disparities begins with recognizing their existence and is sustained by the relentless pursuit of equity and justice.

Let's embrace this challenge not just with words but with deeds, committing to a future where legal systems empower rather than disenfranchise. In the spirit of equity, each step taken towards more inclusive and fair legal frameworks marks progress, reinstating the balance that justice demands.

Ultimately, the question isn't merely about the existence of social inequality within legal systems; it's about our collective willingness to confront and correct these disparities. This chapter may continue through the actions we take, anchoring justice in reality rather than leaving it adrift as an idealistic notion.

Unequal Access to Justice is not just a byproduct of social inequality; it sits at the heart of the struggle for justice in modern legal systems. In today's complex society, the challenge of verifying facts cannot be separated from the conversation about inequity. Information asymmetry and the ability to marshal factual evidence give an advantage to those with resources, exacerbating the divide between the haves and the have-nots, and creating a justice system that often privileges those who can afford to manipulate it.

When discussing the issues of fact verification, it's essential to understand that not everyone has equal access to the tools necessary for effective participation in the legal process. Many marginalized communities find themselves at a disadvantage simply because they lack resources like top-tier legal representation or access to digital tools that facilitate robust fact-checking. The system, therefore, becomes skewed in favor of those who not only have the means but also the know-how to present their version of the truth compellingly. In this way, justice becomes less about the pursuit of truth and more about the strategic presentation of information.

Moreover, the legal complexities surrounding fact verification are often compounded by socioeconomic factors. For instance, impoverished individuals may struggle to understand the intricate processes involved in their legal battles. Often, they're unable to afford expert witnesses or comprehensive investigations that could bolster their claims. This inequity in fact presentation enhances the risk of miscarriages of justice, where verdicts are rendered not based on truth, but on who can construct a more convincing narrative with the resources they possess.

At its core, unequal access to justice is a corrosive force, hollowing out the integrity of legal systems. This reality poses a moral and ethical challenge to society at large. Legal systems, ideally, should function as the ultimate leveler, providing every individual with a fair chance regardless of their background. Instead, these systems frequently mirror and perpetuate the very inequalities they should be challenging. As long as the verification of facts remains a battlefield unequally fought, the broader goals of justice and fairness will remain elusive.

So what can be done to address these disparities? It begins with recognizing the problem and then taking deliberate steps to reform the system. Public policies that democratize access to legal resources and encourage transparency in legal proceedings are essential steps forward. Empowering marginalized communities with tools for effective fact-checking and providing them with equitable legal assistance would help bridge the gap. Engaging in grassroots advocacy to highlight these issues can also instigate broader systemic changes, ultimately aligning the legal system closer to its mission of impartial justice.

The conversation about *Unequal Access to Justice* forces us to confront uncomfortable truths but also offers a path toward reform.

It's an invitation to rethink how legal systems can better serve all individuals, ensuring that justice is not a privilege but a universal right. By addressing the inequities in fact verification, we take a significant step toward a more inclusive and fair legal landscape. Our society's commitment to equality and justice must be unwavering, and it starts with building a legal system that serves everyone fairly and equitably.

The Impact of Socioeconomic Disparities resonates deeply within the framework of social inequality and legal systems, especially in the context of verifying facts. Disparities in wealth and access to resources create a labyrinthine landscape where truth and justice are often obscured. When citizens from different economic backgrounds encounter the legal system, they bring with them unequal abilities to support their claims, which complicates fact-checking and the pursuit of truth. In many cases, wealthier individuals have access to robust legal representation that can afford expensive evidence-gathering processes, while poorer counterparts may struggle with even basic documentation.

The challenge of verifying facts in legal matters exacerbates these socioeconomic divides. Legal systems, ostensibly neutral, are frequently pulled toward those who can navigate them most effectively—which often means those who can pay. This is not only a question of hiring the best lawyers but also a matter of being able to employ private investigators, forensic experts, and other professionals who contribute to building a strong case. These tools and services are luxuries often beyond the reach of the financially disadvantaged, leading to a de facto inequality in the pursuit of justice.

Consider the implications in a criminal case: the accused without resources may face devastating odds against a well-funded state prosecution. The integrity of evidence, the fairness of witness testimony, and even the accuracy of alibis become malleable concepts when money can buy expertise, time, and exhaustive research. The truth-seeking function of the legal system becomes compromised when verifying facts is a privilege, not a right. Resultantly, disparities in socioeconomic status create an uneven playing field where truth is sometimes aligned with financial capability rather than factual accuracy.

Socioeconomic inequality perpetuates itself by limiting access to legal resources and hampering the effectiveness of fact verification in the justice system. This cyclical disadvantage suggests that disparity isn't simply an ancillary issue but a central barrier to equitable justice. As efforts to verify facts become heavily resource-dependent, the system unwittingly favors those who are already advantaged. Consequently, this hierarchy of access fosters mistrust among lower-income communities who perceive—and often rightfully so—that the scales of justice are tipped against them.

At this juncture, addressing the socioeconomic disparities that pervade the justice system is not just about leveling the playing field; it's about ensuring the credibility and integrity of the entire judicial process. When fact verification becomes equitable, when access isn't determined by the dollar sign, we inch closer to a system that champions fair justice. Legal reform, therefore, must involve mechanisms that democratize the process, providing equal opportunities for fact-checking and evidence presentation, irrespective of one's socioeconomic status. In doing so, we don't just address inequality; we uphold the foundational tenets of justice itself.

Chapter 9:
The Role of Education in
Upholding Justice

Education, it's been said, is the cornerstone of a just society. Yet, amid the clamor of today's ever-changing world, it's critical that education extends beyond traditional boundaries. It's not enough to simply impart knowledge; education must also foster critical thinking and a commitment to justice. In a landscape where misinformation can spread like wildfire, the role of education becomes ever more pivotal— not just in classrooms but as a fabric interwoven throughout society.

The decline of truth in legal systems, though lamented, is no longer surprising in our digital age, where the difference between fact and fiction can be dangerously thin. It's in this context that we find the greater mission of education: to arm individuals with the analytical tools necessary to discern truth and uphold ethical principles. The educators of today don't just teach students; they build the architects of justice for tomorrow.

But what does it mean to educate for justice? For one, it involves reshaping the curriculum for aspiring legal practitioners. Legal education often binds itself within the confines of statutes and precedents, but it must reach further. Law schools, in their pursuit of teaching jurisprudential rigor, have a responsibility to pair doctrinal knowledge with practical insights. In the courtroom, as in life, book smarts need to walk hand in hand with street smarts.

Indeed, the challenge goes beyond mere instruction. Schools and universities must nurture a spirit of inquiry that probes beneath the surface of legal codes and into the essence of justice itself. Encouraging students to question, to critique, and to envision better systems is just as vital as learning to parse legal texts. Lawyers and judges of the future must envision themselves not just as interpreters of the law, but as custodians of justice.

Moreover, the challenge of upholding justice isn't confined to those within the legal profession. Public legal literacy is a critical element, too often overlooked, in the quest for a fair and equitable society. As everyday citizens navigate a complex world, an understanding of legal systems empowers them to engage more effectively with structures of power and governance. Knowledge shouldn't be guarded like a treasure but shared openly to nurture an informed populace.

In empowering citizens with legal understanding, we also see power shifting back to the people where it rightly belongs. This doesn't just mean understanding one's rights, but also one's responsibilities. It's about fostering a communal approach to justice where individuals understand their role within the societal web. This interconnectedness, grounded in shared knowledge, is what keeps justice from being a lofty ideal and makes it a living reality.

In our digital age, the role of education in upholding justice becomes ever more nuanced. Interactive platforms, open-access courses, and digital resources democratize access to legal knowledge. This is revolutionary; what once required proximity to brick-and-mortar institutions is now universally accessible. It represents a profound shift, enabling voices from varied backgrounds to join the conversation about justice.

However, technology also poses challenges—misinformation and biased algorithms threaten the integrity of available knowledge.

Ensuring that digital platforms uphold truth and neutrality becomes a mission schools and universities must embrace. In doing so, they must strike a balance between innovation and tradition, between global access and local specificity.

This commitment to justice through education doesn't rest solely within academia. Policymakers have a critical role in forging alliances with educators to create frameworks that prioritize equitable access to quality education. It's about ensuring that resources are available to all, irrespective of their zip code or socioeconomic status. A society aiming at justice can't afford educational disparities.

Throughout history, some of the greatest strides in justice have come from educational reform. Social movements that initially grew from academic centers have sparked widespread change. By planting seeds of critical thought and ethical reasoning, education can ignite a passion for justice that reverberates across society.

One can't overlook the power of storytelling in education. History isn't just a collection of dates and names; it's a narrative filled with lessons. By teaching students the stories behind justice—the struggles, triumphs, and failures—we create a tapestry that resonates far beyond rote memorization. It's about breathing life into the principles of justice, showing both its fragility and its strength through real-world anecdotes.

Ultimately, the role of education in upholding justice is both a responsibility and an opportunity. It's a duty to mold not just capable professionals, but informed citizens who cherish and steward the values of justice in all facets of life. It requires bold steps and transformative ideas, breaking free from archaic molds that might constrain creativity and commitment to true equity and fairness.

The journey toward a just society is long and winding, akin to navigating a river with many tributaries. Education serves as the compass by which the ship of state can find its true course. Whether in fostering the next generation of legal minds or empowering every citizen with knowledge, the aims of justice are none other than shared in the pursuit of education.

Educating Future Legal Practitioners in today's world is an imperative task, particularly when it comes to tackling the challenge of verifying facts. As we confront an era where truth seems more elusive than ever, equipping the next generation of legal professionals with the tools to discern fact from fiction is crucial. The traditional methods of legal education are being tested, as the rapid spread of misinformation through digital channels complicates the legal landscape. So, how do we prepare future practitioners to navigate these turbulent waters?

First, we must broaden the curriculum to reflect the complexities of modern information ecosystems. Law schools should incorporate courses on information literacy and digital forensics, helping students understand the nuances of data in a digital world. With fake news and manipulated data on the rise, legal practitioners need more than just a passing knowledge of these elements. They need to become adept at scrutinizing the reliability of information before it's introduced as evidence in courtrooms.

Moreover, fostering critical thinking skills is just as important as studying case law or statutes. Legal educators must challenge students to question the sources and validity of the information they encounter. A law degree should not only signify proficiency in legal doctrines but also indicate a graduate's ability to navigate the complexities of modern information verification. This means encouraging a mindset that regards skepticism as a tool rather than a hindrance.

Next, let's consider the role of experiential learning. Internships, clinics, and moot courts provide invaluable, hands-on experience where students learn to apply theoretical knowledge to real-world scenarios. These experiences hone the skills required for effective fact-checking and evidence analysis. Students dealing with actual cases will find these opportunities crucial as they help bridge the gap between classroom theory and practical application, giving them a firsthand look at the importance of verifying facts.

Additionally, collaboration with other disciplines can offer fresh perspectives and solutions. Courses that intersect with journalism, computer science, and ethics can expose law students to a broader range of strategies for addressing factual discrepancies. Interdisciplinary approaches can foster innovative solutions for fact verification, drawing from technological advancements and ethical considerations that may be overlooked in traditional legal education.

But we shouldn't stop at academic reforms. The legal community should also encourage ongoing education for practicing attorneys. Workshops and seminars focusing on the latest developments in media literacy, data analysis, and digital privacy should become regular offerings. Continuous education ensures that practicing lawyers remain ahead of the curve, equipped to handle the pervasive waves of misinformation that could sway legal judgments.

In conclusion, the challenge of verifying facts in today's legal systems is formidable, yet it presents an opportunity to redefine legal education for the betterment of justice. By equipping future legal practitioners with the knowledge and skills necessary to tackle misinformation and verify facts with rigor, we lay a solid foundation for justice to not only withstand but thrive amidst the complexities of the modern world.

Public Legal Literacy plays a pivotal role in ensuring justice, especially when society grapples with "The Challenge of Verifying Facts." The essence of public legal literacy lies in its ability to empower individuals to discern truth from misinformation. In a world flooded with information, distinguishing facts from fiction is a crucial skill for maintaining the integrity of legal systems. This skill becomes even more vital as misinformation often shapes public perception and influences legal outcomes. Through education, people can cultivate a sharper understanding of legal processes and the standards of evidence, enhancing their ability to participate meaningfully in democratic governance.

Consider how easily a rumor, even one with a kernel of truth, can spiral into a widely accepted falsehood with far-reaching implications. When the public lacks the tools to critically evaluate legal information, the line between fact and fiction blurs. This erosion of truth can lead to miscarriages of justice, swaying jury verdicts, and influencing judicial opinions. Educational initiatives that focus on improving legal literacy are crucial. They can provide citizens with the capabilities to engage with legal content critically and assess the validity of the information they encounter.

This challenge of verifying facts isn't solely the burden of the courts, but rather a societal responsibility. Every person who understands their rights and obligations under the law is better equipped to resist manipulation and deception. Imagine a society where individuals navigate the complexities of legal systems with confidence and clarity. They'd demand accountability, not just from their leaders, but within their communities, advocating for truth and transparency at every level.

While formal education systems are a natural starting point, they are not the end of the journey. Public campaigns, workshops, and accessible online resources can fortify what formal education has begun, reaching broader audiences. These tools should focus on real-world applications, showing how legal principles intersect with daily life, media consumption, and civic engagement. By turning passive consumers into active participants, education shifts power from the few to the many.

In essence, fostering public legal literacy can dismantle barriers erected by misinformation. As people grow more adept at verifying facts, they contribute to a society that values justice, one that resists the erosion of truth. Viewing education as a constant, evolving effort rather than a temporary fix is vital for long-term change. Let's harness the power of informed citizens, who are unafraid of complexity and critical thinking, to act as the vanguard in upholding justice.

Chapter 10:
Activism and Reform in Legal Systems

The pulverized remnants of outdated legal frameworks scatter across the field of modern activism. With courage and tenacity, individuals and groups blaze pathways toward reform, challenging entrenched systems that serve the few and exclude the many. Activism in legal systems is both a mirror reflecting societal calls for justice and a hammer reshaping the foundations of law. This relentless pursuit of equity isn't just about loud protests or viral hashtags; it's about transforming the dialogue around justice to include voices historically marginalised or altogether silenced.

Grassroots movements often serve as the heartbeat of legal reform. They arise from communities that have endured systemic injustice and have, over time, cultivated a profound understanding of the intricate barriers they face. It's not merely a call for change; it's an assertion of presence, a refusal to be sidelined. These movements demand our attention, bringing a dimension to legal activism that challenges the status quo with relentless precision. Whether through community-led legal clinics or lobbying for policy shifts, grassroots efforts have demonstrated an extraordinary ability to reform systems from the ground up.

Amidst a cacophony of competing interests, policy initiatives emerge as essential tools for systemic change. These initiatives often require navigating complex bureaucracies and confronting entrenched power structures. Yet, when successful, they help codify justice into the law more securely than any pure protest ever could. Policymakers, while sometimes painted as unyielding or disconnected, are crucial allies in this endeavor. By listening to activists and affected communities, they can enact reforms that reflect the diverse tapestry of public needs.

But aligning activism with policy isn't just an academic exercise; it's a high-stakes negotiation where every comma and clause carries weight. The outcomes of these initiatives vary, often depending on the ability of reform advocates to maintain pressure and visibility amid shifting political landscapes. Sometimes, what begins as compromise can grow into robust, far-reaching legislation that stands the test of time, altering the legal terrain in meaningful ways.

It's important to remember that activism and reform are not uniformly welcomed. They are often met with considerable resistance from those who benefit most from the current state of affairs. Legal systems, with their deep roots in tradition, can be sluggish to adapt, if not outright resistant to change. Activists often confront well-funded opposition, derogatory narratives, and cynical punditry trying to paint reform efforts as radical or unnecessary. Yet through determination and solidarity, they persist, igniting broader conversations and recalibrating public consciousness.

Rhetoric plays a profound role in this dynamic. Words have the power to galvanize support, articulate grievances, and frame reform narratives that resonate across demographics. Activists today harness digital tools and social media platforms, crafting messages that transcend geographical and cultural barriers. This virtual activism dovetails with street-level advocacies like protests and legal clinics, creating a synergistic force that disrupts complacency and demands accountability.

Well-documented case studies highlight both triumphs and setbacks in the realm of legal activism. The successes may be marked by the passage of progressive laws or the dismantling of regressive policies, while failures often teach invaluable lessons about coalition-building and strategic planning. Critical to these efforts is the genuine engagement of those most affected by legal inadequacies. Effective advocacy amplifies their voices, translating lived experiences into compelling legal narratives that lawmakers can't ignore.

Particularly inspiring are the stories of individuals whose courage catalyzes collective action. From civil rights leaders to grassroots organizers, history is replete with figures who took monumental risks to challenge unjust laws. Their legacies offer blueprints for contemporary reformers, underscoring the enduring power of individual agency in galvanizing broader societal change.

Collaboration across sectors also makes a significant impact. Legal professionals, academics, and activists, when working in tandem, bring a multifaceted approach to reform. Each brings unique insights and expertise that enrich advocacy efforts, bridging the gap between theoretical insights and practical implementations. This collective intelligence can sever the Gordian knots that hinder legal progress, finding innovative solutions to age-old problems.

While it can be tempting to become cynical about the pace and success of legal reform, it's crucial to recognize the evolution underway. Incremental changes stack up, often unnoticed, until a tipping point causes a visible transformation in the legal landscape. By steadfastly pursuing reform, activists gradually bend the arc of the moral universe toward justice, reminding us that progress, however slow, is undeniably part of our shared human story.

In conclusion, activism and reform in legal systems present one of the most profound opportunities for societal progress. The task demands unyielding dedication, continual learning, and strategic action. As history has shown, while the path is fraught with challenges, it's the unwavering pursuit of justice that brings about profound change. The charge for activists, scholars, and policymakers alike is to carry forward this mission, nurturing the seeds of reform until they bloom into a more equitable and just legal landscape for all.

Grassroots Movements for Change

Grassroots movements have long been the beating heart of activism, pumping vigor and commitment into the veins of stagnant systems. Their resonance in the legal arena is a testament to the indomitable spirit of citizens who refuse to accept injustice as the norm. These movements are like pressure cookers, building steam at the community level until they force real, tangible change in legal systems that too often feel set in stone. Throughout history, what first seems a whisper at the margins frequently swells to a roar, capturing the nation's attention and demanding reform.

Consider how grassroots organizations rise to challenge undue power and inequality within legal frameworks. It's not just about protesting on the streets or holding up signs; it's about mobilizing communities around shared grievances and aspirations. These are the mothers who rally for child welfare reform, the workers who push for equitable labor laws, and the students who advocate for education reform in an outdated justice system. These communities stitch together the fabric of change using creative tactics formed in living rooms, community centers, and online forums. These grassroots efforts channel collective frustration into collective action, often implementing reform from the ground up.

The heart of grassroots movements lies in their approach, which contrasts sharply with top-down policy initiatives. Where governmental reforms might take years, burdened by bureaucracy and often diluted by compromise, grassroots movements act with immediacy and focus. They're not waiting for an invitation to make a seat at the table; they're already setting it and inviting everyone willing to listen and act. It's this tenacity and clear-headed resolve that turns small ripples into tidal waves of systemic shift.

The methods adopted by grassroots movements can differ greatly, yet all share a common foundation: empowerment of the individual to incite broader change. Some movements thrive on community organizing, bringing people together to share stories and strategize. Others might focus intensively on legal advocacy, equipping citizens with knowledge and tools to challenge injustices through judicial systems. Still, others might sway public opinion through the arts or social media campaigns, leveraging the digital age to amplify voices that were once silenced by distance and circumstance.

Don't be fooled: grassroots isn't synonymous with informal or unplanned. Many of these movements are meticulously organized, utilizing the talents and passions of community members who each bring something unique to the table. Whether they're volunteering their legal expertise, providing a platform for storytelling, or supervising logistics, each member plays a vital part in orchestrating change.

Moreover, the power of today's grassroots movements is amplified by technology, which breaks down traditional barriers and connects activists across not only regions but nations. Social media and digital communication serve as the great equalizers, placing the potential for mass mobilization into the hands of anyone with a message and the determination to see it spread. Movements that once would have fought in isolation now find solidarity and a shared struggle with counterparts far and wide, allowing for a more cohesive and unified push for reform.

Yet, grassroots activism faces significant challenges, with barriers often rooted in the very systems they seek to alter. Funding can be scarce, and maintaining momentum is a constant struggle against competing interests and apathy. Moreover, activists often encounter legal and institutional pushback, as established systems resist change that threatens the status quo. But herein lies the mettle of grassroots action—the unyielding resolve to stand up against seemingly insurmountable odds and inspire others to do the same.

Take the example of the civil rights movements—a pivotal reminder of what concerted grassroots effort can accomplish. These collective actions transformed societal norms through sheer perseverance and strategic brilliance. Activists mobilized across demographics and borders, shaking the foundations of discriminatory laws and asserting that change was not only possible but inevitable. This legacy endures, energizing contemporary movements for police reform, LGBTQ+ rights, and climate justice.

In places where legal systems are struggling to adapt to modern challenges, grassroots movements often serve as the voice of reform. From neighborhoods in New York rallying for police accountability to villages in India fighting for environmental protection, these movements bring forth issues that might otherwise remain invisible in political discourse. They're the embodiment of democracy in action, proving that the people don't just have a say—they have the power to redesign the playing field.

But the potency of grassroots movements isn't just about results; it's also about the processes they embody and impart. Participatory action fosters an inclusive vision of justice, where reform isn't dispensed from on high but emerges from the hands of those who live and breathe its implications every day. The education and empowerment gained through such engagement have ripple effects, nurturing civic responsibility and instilling a lasting commitment to communal well-being.

Ultimately, grassroots movements serve as the conscience of societies, a persistent reminder of where we're failing and how we can do better. They inject innovation and passion into legal reforms, challenging outdated norms and clearing the way for more responsive and equitable justice systems. Activism at the grassroots level teaches us that real change often begins with everyday individuals who refuse to accept the status quo. It's a story not just of triumphs but also of the continuous fight for a just world, perpetually reframing the narrative of what justice can be.

As we ponder the future of our legal systems, the question remains: who will be the torchbearers lighting the path to reform? The answer, it seems, lies in the resolute spirits of grassroots movements—the unyielding advocates of change who refuse to be silenced until justice is truly served for all.

Policy Initiatives and Their Outcomes occupy a profound place within the narrative of reform, particularly when driven by grassroots movements. These policy initiatives frequently emerge from the ground up, fueled by the collective effort of communities who envision a fairer and more just legal system. There's an undeniable power in the hands of everyday citizens tirelessly advocating for reforms. Whether they're battling outdated laws or lobbying for new legislation, these grassroots campaigns often serve as the catalyst for vital policy changes, yet they don't always achieve their intended outcomes.

Starting at the community level, grassroots activism often targets issues that seem impervious to reform through traditional channels. These movements gather momentum and gradually command the attention of policymakers. For instance, initiatives aimed at ending mass incarceration or promoting restorative justice aren't merely local demands—they become national conversations that challenge the status quo. When policy changes do occur as a result of such grassroots initiatives, it's crucial to evaluate their effectiveness and sustainability.

Sometimes, these movements inspire legislative bodies to propose and enact new laws that reshape the landscape of justice. In some cases, reforms like decriminalization of non-violent offenses or establishment of accountability boards for law enforcement stem directly from grassroots pressures. While these changes often face initial resistance, they can lead to transformative shifts in how justice is perceived and administered. However, the journey from policy proposal to tangible outcome is fraught with hurdles, including political opposition and bureaucratic inertia.

The success of these policy initiatives depends significantly on endurance and adaptability. As reforms are implemented, unintended consequences can emerge, requiring constant assessment and recalibration. For example, policies designed to enhance community policing might inadvertently strain resources or encounter resistance from within police forces. It becomes essential for activists to remain vigilant, ensuring that these policies are applied equitably and effectively, so the original spirit of the grassroots movement is not lost in translation.

Despite the obstacles, the impact of grassroots movements on policy outcomes can't be overstated. Their strength lies in persistence and their ability to adapt strategies in response to evolving challenges. Policy successes often inspire subsequent movements, creating a ripple effect that extends beyond the original scope. These initiatives, powered by collective will and a compelling vision for justice, establish precedents that other reformers can build upon. However, it's important to recognize that not all movements achieve their desired policy outcomes immediately. Patience, perseverance, and relentless advocacy remain key components to lasting change in the legal landscape.

In summary, grassroots movements play a pivotal role in advancing policy initiatives within legal systems. Such movements, despite facing numerous challenges, have historically been instrumental in initiating reforms that the system initially resists. To ensure these reforms yield positive outcomes, continuous engagement and oversight are necessary from the communities that gave birth to them. While not every initiative achieves success, the journey itself contributes to a broader discourse on justice, serving as a reminder that power truly resides in the voice of the people.

Chapter 11:
Rebuilding the Pillars of Justice

As change sweeps through global societies, the pillars of justice face profound challenges. The task of rebuilding these pillars is urgent and complex. We've explored the erosion of these structures, but now the question is: how do we restore them? To initiate meaningful reform, a multifaceted approach is necessary. The fight to rejuvenate our legal systems requires that truth sits at its core, societal trust is restored, and innovation is embraced.

The first strategy in this endeavor is addressing the erosion of trust between the public and legal institutions. Legal systems are built not just on statutes but on the faith people place in them. This trust has been compromised by numerous factors: political interference, media sensationalism, and the growing influence of misinformation. Restoring trust requires transparency. Courts and legal entities must adopt policies that encourage openness. Public legal literacy initiatives can play a critical role here by enlightening the populace about legal processes and rights, effectively demystifying the justice system.

Moreover, embracing technological innovation is instrumental in this rebuilding process. Digital advancements offer incredible tools to enhance transparency and accessibility. Consider the use of blockchain for secure, unalterable public records or AI to improve the efficiency and consistency of legal proceedings. However, innovation is a double-edged sword. It can facilitate progress while posing new challenges like data privacy concerns. Regulations must adapt swiftly, ensuring technology serves justice rather than undermining it.

Education stands as a primary pillar in rebuilding effective justice systems. A well-informed public is more likely to engage with and trust the laws that govern them. Educational reforms must target both future legal professionals and the general public. For practitioners, curricula should include comprehensive training on emerging technologies and ethical dilemmas. For the public, resources should be made widely available to increase awareness of legal rights and processes.

But even the best systems falter without accountability. Integral to this is a robust system of checks and balances. Accountability mechanisms must be revisited and strengthened, ensuring that those in power cannot manipulate the system for personal gain. Here, international cooperation might offer innovative solutions. By learning from other countries and even cooperating on cross-border issues, we can forge pathways that uphold accountability.

Grassroots movements can't be ignored in this equation. They have historically driven significant change, highlighting public dissatisfaction and advocating for necessary reforms. These movements give voice to marginalized communities, ensuring that their needs are heard and addressed. Policymakers should engage with these groups actively, fostering participatory governance and legitimizing their role in the justice process.

While tackling the structural, our moral compass should also steer reform efforts. Justice should not merely be a legal right but a societal practice upheld by shared values. Emphasizing ethics within legal education and practice is crucial. Encouraging a culture of empathy within the legal system, where the human element is prioritized, helps fortify justice's foundation.

Ultimately, the rebuilding of justice's pillars hinges on these concerted efforts. It demands courage from every participant, from policymakers who draft reforms to the global citizenry who demand them. To forge a future justice system that truly serves its people, all stakeholders must engage in this restorative journey, embracing both innovation and tradition, transparency and accountability, education and activism.

However, the real magic lies in collective action. No single entity or approach can repair a system this complex. It's a mosaic built piece by piece, leveraging the strengths and insights of a diverse society. As we advance in rebuilding these pillars of justice, let's remember that our actions today will define the legacy of justice for generations to come.

Strategies for Restoring Trust To rebuild the pillars of justice, we must first address the critical issue of trust that has eroded over time. Trust is the glue that holds societies together, especially when it comes to our legal systems. At the grassroots level, movements are pivotal in restoring this trust, as they directly engage communities and foster a sense of ownership in the justice process. These movements act as catalysts for change, challenging existing structures and advocating for more accountability and transparency in legal institutions.

Grassroots movements thrive on the notion of empowerment. They offer individuals a platform to voice their concerns and participate in the formation of more equitable systems. One effective strategy these movements employ is community-based restorative justice programs. Unlike traditional punitive approaches, restorative justice seeks to repair harms by involving all stakeholders in a dialogue, aiming for rehabilitation rather than retribution. This kind of participatory justice not only addresses grievances but also re-establishes trust by demonstrating a commitment to fairness and healing.

Engagement is key, and it starts with education. Grassroots organizations often focus on educating the public about their rights and the legal processes that affect their daily lives. By spreading awareness, they dismantle the barriers of ignorance and fear, which are substantial contributors to public distrust. Educational initiatives can take many forms, including workshops, seminars, and even online platforms that reach a broader audience. When people are informed, they are more likely to engage confidently with the justice system, feeling assured that they aren't just cogs in an intimidating machine.

Moreover, these movements often leverage technology to increase transparency and promote accountability. For instance, open data initiatives can make court proceedings and legal documentation more accessible to the public. By keeping citizens informed and involved, transparency can diminish the suspicion that the legal system operates in secrecy or serves only the privileged. Promising applications of blockchain technology are also being explored to create tamper-proof records and fight corruption, ensuring that justice is not only done but seen to be done.

Another effective approach involves forming coalitions. Grassroots organizations often find strength in numbers by joining forces with other advocacy groups, NGOs, and proactive legal professionals. Such alliances enhance their influence and resource bases, enabling them to promote reforms effectively. The combined efforts reinforce public confidence, showcasing diverse but united voices calling for change.

Lastly, it's important to remember that grassroots movements aren't a panacea but a significant step in the right direction. They cannot single-handedly overhaul the system, but they stimulate dialogue, challenge complacency, and illuminate pathways to improve public relations with legal institutions. These movements remind us that the justice system belongs to everyone and urge us to reclaim it as an entity that genuinely serves the public good.

Legal Innovations for the Future As we're poised on the brink of transformation, it's clear that traditional legal frameworks must adapt to remain effective in a rapidly evolving world. In the arena of grassroots movements for change, the potential for legal innovations is being both shaped and tested. What's happening at the community level often serves as the crucible for new ideas, with local activists spearheading changes that resonate on a broader scale. Policy frameworks that are nimble, inclusive, and tech-savvy might be our biggest allies in crafting a justice system that not only serves today but anticipates tomorrow.

Grassroots movements thrive on the conviction that change begins locally. These efforts are all about empowering individuals to challenge institutional inertia. Legal innovations emerging from these movements often prioritize accessibility and transparency. Consider the idea of community courts that operate not just as places of judgment but as arenas of reconciliation and restoration. Such initiatives underscore the shift from purely punitive justice to one that acknowledges the potential for healing and rehabilitation. We can draw from these grassroots blueprints to inform broader legal reforms, creating systems that citizens trust and can navigate with confidence.

Technology, too, is at the forefront of legal change, serving both as a tool and a challenge. The use of blockchain, for instance, to record property rights or contractual obligations ensures consistency and security, providing a permanent and tamper-proof record. Real-time translation services can help bridge language barriers in court, making legal processes more inclusive. But let's not be naïve—even as technology simplifies some aspects, it complicates others. Issues of data privacy and cybersecurity loom large, reminding us that these tools must be wielded with care to avoid pitfalls.

Imagine legal systems marked by laws that are not just reactive but proactively designed with early warning systems for social unrest or injustice. Predictive analytics could identify patterns that signal potential crises, prompting preemptive measures. Such a system encourages a shift from a focus on crime and punishment to one of prevention and well-being. This doesn't just enhance efficiency; it embodies justice with a human face, one that's mindful of social challenges and equipped to address them before they escalate.

These innovative approaches won't materialize in a vacuum. They require collaborative efforts among policymakers, legal experts, and the very communities they are meant to serve. Building a robust, future-ready legal system involves marrying the wisdom of experience with the vitality of new ideas. It's about weaving together diverse perspectives to forge pathways that are resilient, adaptable, and inherently just. After all, the goal is a transformation that is not simply reactive but visionary, ensuring justice remains not a relic of the past but a living, evolving ideal for future generations.

Chapter 12:
The Global Movement
Toward Justice Renewal

The quest for justice is akin to a river that has flowed through human history, shaping our societies, cultures, and governments. Today, this river is facing new obstacles and challenges as we navigate the complex global landscape. The call for justice renewal is a clarion call—a demand from individuals and communities worldwide who seek a system that is fair, equitable, and adaptable to the changes and challenges of the 21st century. As a global community, we are recognizing the urgent need for collaboration across borders, cultures, and legal traditions to address these challenges.

The global movement toward justice renewal is not a singular entity but rather a collection of diverse efforts converging upon a common goal. It acknowledges the inadequacies and inequities that have persisted within legal systems and aims to address them through cooperative action and shared innovation. From grassroots movements to international bodies, the tide is turning towards an understanding that justice is not just an ideal but a practical necessity for global stability and peace.

At the heart of this movement is the realization that justice systems, long thought to be the bedrock of societal order, are under strain. Major challenges, such as the rise of misinformation, political interference, and technological disruption, highlighted in previous chapters, have exposed vulnerabilities. These issues transcend national borders, making international cooperation pivotal. Legal systems must evolve to meet the demands of a digital age while maintaining fundamental principles of fairness and impartiality.

International organizations, such as the United Nations and the International Criminal Court, are playing crucial roles in fostering dialogue and collaboration between nations. These bodies serve as platforms for discussion, development, and implementation of policies aimed at reinforcing legal structures worldwide. Through treaties, conventions, and joint initiatives, they work to harmonize legal standards and practices across different jurisdictions, ensuring that justice systems are not only robust but also resilient.

Furthermore, there is a growing recognition of the importance of drawing from a wide array of cultural perspectives to enrich the global conversation on justice renewal. Indigenous legal traditions, for instance, offer invaluable insights into community-based adjudication and restorative practices. These approaches, which emphasize healing and reconciliation, are gaining traction as complementary methods to conventional punitive systems. By integrating such perspectives, a more holistic and inclusive model of justice can emerge.

Education emerges as another critical pillar in the pursuit of justice renewal. Equipping future generations with a deep understanding of legal principles and human rights is fundamental to driving change. Educational institutions around the world are expanding curricula to include global justice issues, encouraging students to think beyond their own borders. This not only prepares a new era of legal practitioners but also fosters a more informed and engaged citizenry.

Technology, while initially perceived as a disruptor, also presents unprecedented opportunities for justice renewal. Digital platforms and tools can facilitate access to legal resources, streamline judicial processes, and enhance transparency. For instance, blockchain technology is already being explored to secure evidence chains and ensure the integrity of legal transactions. Artificial intelligence, if wielded ethically, can aid in case management and decision-making, reducing backlog and enhancing efficiency.

However, the path toward justice renewal is fraught with challenges. To harness the potential of these transformative forces, it is imperative to address disparities and imbalances that persist both within and between nations. There is a critical need for equitable access to technology and resources. Without addressing these issues, the digital divide could widen, exacerbating existing inequalities and undermining efforts to create a fair global justice framework.

The role of civil societies and citizen-led initiatives cannot be overstated in this global movement. Activists and NGOs continue to push for reforms, highlighting issues such as corruption, human rights abuses, and unequal access to justice. Their efforts are instrumental in applying pressure on governments and international bodies to enact meaningful change. These grassroots movements provide a crucial counterbalance to institutional inertia, keeping the momentum for justice renewal alive and dynamic.

The notion of justice renewal also extends to environmental justice, recognizing the interconnectedness of legal systems and ecological sustainability. Policies and legal frameworks are evolving to incorporate environmental considerations, acknowledging the rights of nature and the need for sustainable development. This expansion of the justice mandate reflects a broader understanding of the inextricable link between human rights and environmental stewardship in ensuring the well-being of future generations.

Looking forward, the global movement toward justice renewal is poised to grow stronger as more stakeholders join the cause. The path ahead must be navigated with care, collaboration, and a commitment to shared values. By dismantling barriers, embracing diverse perspectives, and prioritizing equity and inclusion, the world can craft a justice system that not only responds to present challenges but also evolves to meet future needs.

In conclusion, the global movement toward justice renewal is a testament to humanity's enduring pursuit of fairness and equity. It calls for a reimagining of justice systems to make them more inclusive, transparent, and adaptive. As concerned citizens, legal scholars, and policymakers, we must rise to this challenge, ensuring that justice is not just an aspiration but a reality for all. Together, through collective effort and unwavering resolve, we can build a future where justice truly serves and uplifts everyone.

Collaborative International Efforts are emerging as a cornerstone in building a more equitable global justice system. In the complex web of global interconnectedness, grassroots movements are standing out as powerful catalysts for change. From small community gatherings to large-scale international alliances, these efforts are reshaping the landscape of justice and calling for an end to systems that leave many marginalized and unheard.

It's not just about seeking justice within national borders anymore; it's about crafting a vision that transcends them. Countries are recognizing that the challenges of inequality, corruption, and systemic bias can't be solved in isolation. As a result, we're seeing a wave of international collaborations designed to address these concerns. These collaborations are creating networks that span continents, leveraging diverse perspectives and expertise to tackle shared issues. By uniting on a global scale, they amplify the voices of those at the front lines of grassroots movements, ensuring that their cries for reform are heard louder and clearer than ever.

Grassroots movements have historically been the undercurrent of larger societal changes, often sparking from local injustices that resonate on a broader scale. As these movements gain momentum, they're increasingly reaching across borders. Initiatives like community-driven research collaborations, cross-border advocacy, and international justice forums are gaining traction, drawing support from not only policymakers but also ordinary citizens who want to see real change. By working together, these movements are starting to influence global policies and initiatives aimed at justice renewal.

This international focus is not just an alliance of governments or legal scholars; it's a tapestry of diverse groups committed to a common mission. These efforts highlight the strength of unity, where different cultures and systems can teach each other the best practices while respecting individual sovereignty. One profound outcome of these collaborations is the sharing of successful grassroots strategies that have worked on the local level. This exchange transforms isolated victories into a global toolkit of effective solutions. Countries with historically entrenched issues of legal inequality are finding fresh inspiration and practical strategies through these shared experiences.

Moreover, technology is playing a pivotal role in these collaborative efforts. Digital platforms are providing unprecedented opportunities for knowledge exchange, bringing together activists, scholars, and policymakers from all corners of the globe. Online campaigns, virtual conferences, and international webinars are breaking down geographical barriers, allowing for a more seamless sharing of ideas and strategies. This tech-fueled collaboration is enabling rapid dissemination of information, helping movements grow and adapt in real-time.

What's clear is that collaborative international efforts are not a mere trend but a critical pathway toward justice renewal. They fuel hope and action, illustrating how collective resolve can create more transparent and fair systems globally. It's an ongoing journey, one propelled by the belief that through solidarity and shared purpose, justice can be reimagined and achieved for all. By continuing to foster these partnerships, we're building a future where justice knows no borders, grounded in the simple yet powerful principle that together, we are stronger.

The Path Forward represents a beacon of hope in the ongoing struggle for justice renewal, particularly through grassroots movements for change. These movements have proven that profound change often blossoms from the ground up, driven by individuals and communities motivated by a shared vision for a fairer world. Some might say the key to unlocking widespread reform lies within these passionate collectives, each one a vital cog in the machinery of justice.

It's imperative we recognize the strength and innovation that grassroots movements bring to the table. Unlike larger bureaucratic entities that often get bogged down in red tape, these local groups operate with agility, responding dynamically to the pressing needs of their communities. They harness the power and immediacy of lived experiences to craft initiatives that resonate deeply and address specific injustices at a local level. By amplifying diverse voices, they catalyze change that is not only powerful but remarkably sustainable.

However, to forge a successful path forward, grassroots movements must cultivate symbiotic relationships with policymakers and legal scholars. Bridging the gap between formal legal structures and community-driven initiatives can be a daunting task, but it is not insurmountable. Building alliances with academic and governmental bodies provides the scaffolding necessary for these movements to thrive on larger stages. Support from institutions can magnify their efforts, lending the resources and legitimacy that help propel community-driven change into the legal mainstream.

Moreover, technology plays an essential role in amplifying grassroots efforts. We are living in a digital age where mobilizing more significant numbers and spreading awareness can happen at the click of a button. Leveraging social media, crowdfunding platforms, and other digital tools ensures that movements can expand their reach and impact, gaining support from like-minded individuals across the globe. Technology not only facilitates wider reach but also promotes transparency and accountability, crucial components in building trust with broader audiences.

As we look toward the horizon, the challenge lies in maintaining the grassroots ethos of authenticity and genuine commitment while expanding its reach and influence. This balancing act requires continuous engagement and empowerment of community members to ensure that the core issues remain centered around the individuals most affected by them. It also demands adaptable strategies capable of addressing both present and emerging challenges.

The path forward is undoubtedly laden with obstacles, yet it is equally filled with the promise of transformation. By valuing and integrating the insights offered by grassroots movements, we can begin to reshape justice systems to reflect the diverse tapestry of the societies they are meant to serve. Ultimately, the journey toward a renewed conception of justice is a shared endeavor, requiring persistence, collaboration, and an unwavering belief in the potential for meaningful change.

Conclusion

As we draw this examination of justice and legal systems to a close, we find ourselves at a significant crossroads. The insights and analyses throughout the preceding chapters reveal a complex tapestry of challenges and opportunities. It's clear that the dynamics of justice have shifted dramatically, shaped by social, political, and technological forces in ways that our predecessors might never have envisioned. It's no longer adequate to merely understand these transformations; proactive steps are essential to preserve the integrity and efficacy of legal systems.

The erosion of foundational legal principles isn't just an intellectual concern affecting legal scholars and policymakers—it's a pressing issue that impacts every corner of society. When truth becomes precarious in the courts, and justice is perceived as a privilege rather than a right, public trust deteriorates. This trust, once fractured, is exceedingly difficult to restore. It's crucial that the role of truth in law is reestablished as the bedrock of justice, for without it, the legal framework weakens, jeopardizing the very fabric of society.

It's the role of each concerned citizen to ensure that the law remains an unwavering anchor amidst social turbulence. Truth mustn't bend under the weight of misinformation, nor should public perception be swayed by skewed narratives. The media and its portrayal of legal proceedings wield considerable influence—one that calls for both skepticism and critical engagement from the public. Justice mustn't be left solely in the hands of those within the system;

rather, it thrives when cultivated through active and informed public participation.

International perspectives shed light on both pitfalls and triumphs in justice systems globally. They remind us that despite different legal landscapes, common themes of disparity and inequality ring true, compelling a global dialogue toward equitable solutions. Countries might adopt varied approaches to justice, but collaboration strengthens the resolve to uphold human rights and dignity across borders. As we step into a more interconnected world, international partnerships seem more vital than ever in safeguarding and reforming legal systems.

Technology, a double-edged sword, brings both evolution and complexity to justice. While it offers unprecedented tools and potential benefits, it also poses formidable challenges to legal precedent and fact verification. The integration of digital evidence and artificial intelligence into courtrooms demands vigilance and adaptability. These advancements must serve justice—not supersede it, unimpaired by biases or inequities embedded in algorithms. Legal practitioners must advocate for transparency and fairness in the use of technology within the judiciary.

Restoring faith in the legal system hinges on addressing political influence and social inequality head-on. The intersection of law and politics is fraught with instances of interference that threaten legal integrity. Moreover, substantial disparities in access to justice reinforce cycles of disadvantage. Concerted efforts and grassroots activism play a crucial role in leveling the playing field, pushing for policies that bridge the gap between the advantaged and the marginalized.

Education emerges as a cornerstone in sustaining justice. For both future legal practitioners and the general public, a robust legal education fuels a principled and informed citizenry. When people understand their rights and the responsibilities of the legal system, they are empowered to hold it accountable. This empowerment is the seed from which justice reform can grow, safeguarding democracy and fostering a culture of accountability.

As we consider the future, the question is not just how we address these contemporary challenges, but how we shape a legacy of legal systems that are inclusive, transparent, and resilient. Policy initiatives and legal innovations are merely the first steps. Sustaining momentum requires an enduring commitment to principles of fairness and justice. This path forward, though fraught with challenges, calls for unified action and a shared vision—a world where justice is not an aspiration, but a lived reality.

The global movement toward justice renewal signifies hope and commitment. Collaborative efforts across nations reaffirm that justice is a collective endeavor, transcending beyond borders. The path is neither simple nor assured, but with determination and unity, it remains within reach. Let's strive to rebuild and renew, fueled by the belief that justice is the compass guiding communities toward equality and peace.

Appendix A:
Additional Resources

This appendix aims to provide a robust starting point for anyone eager to delve deeper into the complex and evolving field of justice and legal systems. While the chapters have taken us through various nuances—from misinformation's impact on legal integrity to the intricate dance between law and politics—it's evident that the journey doesn't end here. Whether you're a concerned citizen, a legal scholar, or a policymaker, the resources listed below are selected to further inspire action and understanding in your pursuit of justice reform.

Books and Articles

- *The Collapse of American Criminal Justice* by William J. Stuntz - This book offers a critical analysis of the U.S. criminal justice system, providing historical insights and examining contemporary challenges.

- *Just Mercy* by Bryan Stevenson - A compelling account of Stevenson's work as a lawyer fighting on behalf of marginalized communities, it's an inspiring read for understanding the human elements of justice.

- "Legal Systems Very Different From Ours" by David Friedman - An engaging exploration of alternative legal systems that can expand perspectives on how justice is administered globally.

Organizations and Institutes

- **The Innocence Project** - Committed to exonerating wrongly convicted individuals, this organization provides substantial resources on legal reform.

- **American Civil Liberties Union (ACLU)** - Focused on defending individual rights, the ACLU offers research materials and guides on constitutional laws and practices.

- **World Justice Project** - This global organization publishes the World Justice Index, shedding light on how the rule of law is experienced across countries.

Online Platforms and Courses

- **Coursera and edX** - Offering a variety of courses related to law and justice, these educational platforms provide access to lectures from leading universities.

- **Harvard Law Review Online** - A resource for critical legal scholarship, featuring articles that address the modern challenges facing legal systems.

- **Lawfare Blog** - An excellent source for commentary and analysis on hard national security choices, impacting both law and policy.

Podcasts and Videos

- **Serial** - This groundbreaking podcast examines justice through real-life cases, offering listeners an in-depth look into the American legal system.

- **Justice in America** - A podcast that demystifies the justice system, focusing on its impact on everyday lives.

- **TED Talks related to Law** - Engaging presentations on various aspects of law, justice, and societal impact, these talks are thought-provoking and informative.

Exploring these resources can enrich your perspective and equip you with the tools needed to address the changing dynamics of justice. Whether you're crafting policies, educating future practitioners, or mobilizing community efforts, the path toward justice renewal begins with informed action.

www.ingramcontent.com/pod-product-compliance
Lightning Source LLC
Chambersburg PA
CBHW030410290526
45785CB00004B/1960